MANY members
yet ONE body

Committed Same-Gender Relationships
and the Mission of the Church

Craig L. Nessan

Augsburg Fortress
Minneapolis

MANY MEMBERS, YET ONE BODY
Committed Same-Gender Relationships and the Mission of the Church

Unless otherwise stated, Scripture quotations are from New Revised Standard Version Bible, copyright © 1989 Division of Christian Education of the National Council of the Churches of Christ in the United States of America. Used by permission.

Scripture quotations on pages 59 and 68 are from *The New Testament and Psalms: An Inclusive Version* (New York: Oxford University Press, 1995).

Editors: Vicky Goplin and James Satter
Cover Design: Robert Warren Carlson, Minneapolis Design
Cover Photo: PhotoDisc, copyright © 2004
Text Design: James Satter

ISBN 0-8066-4903-8

The paper used in this publication meets the minimum requirements of American National Standard for Information Sciences—Permanence of Paper for Printed Library Materials, ANSI Z329.48-1984.

Manufactured in the U.S.A.

12   11   10   09   08   07   06   05   04   2   3   4   5   6   7   8   9

Contents

Preface

From its very origins, the Christian church has been a fragile and fractious community. It is no small comfort to me that we have from the apostle Paul in the New Testament his correspondence with one of the most contentious churches of all time. While it may feel that the issues we face are more troublesome than ever before, Paul's letters to the church in Corinth teach us that every generation, beginning with the first, has had its share of controversies that seem to have no promise of resolution. The threat of schism is always near at hand. Yet after nearly 2,000 years of strife, the church of Jesus Christ continues to live.

The most terrifying issues for many people in the church today swirl around the topic of homosexuality: How should the church relate to gay and lesbian persons? How should we minister to their families? Is homosexuality a sin? What does the Bible say about it? How should we in the church assess our culture's opinions about homosexuality? How can Christians hold such opposite views on this subject? And then there are the two questions that are the central focus of this book:

1. Should the Evangelical Lutheran Church in America allow for the blessing of committed same-gender relationships?

2. Should the ELCA allow the ordination/rostering of otherwise qualified candidates who are living in a committed same-gender relationship?

We encounter many fears when we begin to think about these questions and especially when the church takes up a study of them. When I began my study of homosexuality some years ago, I believed that the topic was primarily about matters of human sexuality. Studying Scripture carefully and paying attention to the findings of modern science will lead us to the answers we are looking for.

4

In this book, I am committed to offering my best understanding of the biblical witness and my most thorough reasoning about the particular questions before us. What I have discovered, however, is that our discussion of this particular issue has as much to do with ecclesiology as it does with sexuality. As we enter into pointed debate about an issue so hotly contested, we are challenged to examine our core commitments about the nature of the church. What does it mean to be church together with people with whom I vehemently disagree? What suffices as the basis for the unity of the church? How much difference of opinion is permissible, before we have betrayed the truth? Thus this book is not only about homosexuality but also ecclesiology.

This book makes frequent reference to the apostle Paul's first letter to the church in Corinth. In Paul's message to that church, I find much that desperately needs to be heard by the church today, as we negotiate our way through the controversies that confound us. The title for the book, *Many Members, Yet One Body*, is taken from 1 Corinthians 12:20. In the passage below, we hear this verse in the larger context of 1 Corinthians 12:14-26. This text sets the tone for what I think we need to claim about the nature of the church in our time. This is especially true as we face controversies that are just as menacing as the ones in the first century:

> Indeed, the body does not consist of one member but many. If the foot would say, "Because I am not a hand, I do not belong to the body," that would not make it any less a part of the body. And if the ear would say, "Because I am not an eye, I do not belong to the body," that would not make it any less a part of the body. If the whole body were an eye, where would the hearing be? If the whole body were hearing, where would the sense of smell be? But as it is, God arranged the members in the body, each one of them, as [God] chose. If all were a single member, where would the body be? As it is, there are many members, yet one body. The eye cannot say to the hand, "I have no need of you," nor again the head to the feet, "I have no need of you." On the contrary, the members of the body that

seem to be weaker are indispensable, and those members of the body that we think less honorable we clothe with greater honor, and our less respectable members are treated with greater respect; whereas our more respectable members do not need this. But God has so arranged the body, giving the greater honor to the inferior member, that there be no dissension within the body, but the members may have the same care for one another. If one member suffers, all suffer together with it; if one member is honored, all rejoice together with it. Now you are the body of Christ and individually members of it.

— 1 Corinthians 12:14-26, NRSV

I know no other text that needs to become woven into the fabric of our life as a church in the next years as this one. Paul's ancient wisdom to the church of Corinth as it faced divisive issues is the very same wisdom urgently needed by our church. Jesus Christ makes us members of a single body, whether we like it or not.

The questions accompanying each chapter offer potential for using this book for individual reflection or group discussion. Each of the six chapters is graced with a hymn text that has been sung on the several occasions when I have delivered these pages as lectures. I encourage study groups to consider singing these wonderful hymns wherever people gather to discuss the themes of this book. The hymns were selected for their value in keeping our eyes focused on the mission of the church, especially when controversy threatens to divert us from that mission. Chapter 5 offers detailed suggestions for designing a study process. If you are in charge of leading a study group based on the book, you may find it helpful to read this chapter at the outset. The bibliography selects titles from a wide variety of perspectives that I commend to readers for further study.

As I began presenting my views on homosexuality and the church as set forth in this book, I had no inkling how they would be received. Many routinely have offered their condolences when they heard this was the topic of a recent speaking engagement. I can honestly say that my interactions with church members and leaders around the themes of this book have provided the most awesome speaking engagements of my teaching career. There is far more good will in our church to find a way through the questions surrounding homosexuality than I ever could have imagined. This experience gives me hope for the future of the church, not that we will all agree but that we will find a way to be church together in spite of our disagreements.

Acknowledgments

I would like to thank Pastor Karen Behling and Bishop Harold Usgaard of the Southeastern Minnesota Synod, and Bishop Murray Frick and Pastor Gordon Peterson of the Pacifica Synod, both synods of the Evangelical Lutheran Church in America, for the invitations to speak that became the initial impetus for this book. I have greatly benefited from the conversation with leaders in these and now also several other synods of the church in the process of writing, as well as from students and colleagues at Wartburg Theological Seminary. I am grateful to my colleague in teaching Church and Ministry, Professor Norma Cook Everist, for consultation on the reflection and discussion questions that accompany each of the chapters, and want to express my appreciation to Mary McDermott, our faculty secretary, for assistance in processing the manuscript. At Augsburg Fortress, I am thankful to Beth Lewis, Michael West, Bill Huff, Vicky Goplin, and James Satter for their respective contributions.

This book is written in honor of the family in which I was born and raised. My family of origin has taught me profound lessons about life. Many of them I did not want to learn. Yet I trust that God in Christ has a way of redeeming it all. In gratitude for the joys and the sorrows, I dedicate this book in love to Margaret, Lee, Lucy, John, Nana, Kirk, Kristin, and Marcie. To God be the glory!

ALL SAINTS DAY 2003

Bind Us Together

With One Voice # 748

Refrain
Bind us together, Lord,
bind us together
with cords that cannot be broken.
Bind us together, Lord,
bind us together, Lord;
bind us together in love.

There is only one God.
There is only one King.
There is only one Body;
that is why we can sing:

Refrain

You are the fam'ly of God.
You are the promise divine.
You are God's chosen desire,
you are the glorious new wine.

Refrain

Text: Bob Gillman, b. 1946. Copyright ©
1977 Thankyou Music, admin. (in Western
Hemisphere) Integrity's Hosanna! Music.
Used by permission.

1

The Ultimate
and the Penultimate

CAN THE CENTER HOLD?

Renowned Irish poet William Butler Yeats prophetically cap-
tured the tenor of the emerging postmodern age in the first
stanza of his poem "The Second Coming":

> Turning and turning in the widening gyre
> The falcon cannot hear the falconer;
> Things fall apart; the centre cannot hold;
> Mere anarchy is loosed upon the world,
> The blood-dimmed tide is loosed, and everywhere
> The ceremony of innocence is drowned;
> The best lack all convictions, while the worst
> Are full of passionate intensity. [1]

> — W. B. Yeats (1865-1939)

It is not just the falcon called "society," but even the falcon called
"the church" that no longer easily perceives the voice of the falconer.
When the center no longer holds, things fall apart. Without a central focus, anarchy tears apart God's world. Who remains innocent?
No one I know. No wonder so many people—"the best?"—become
apathetic, while the media is populated by loud, intense voices, each
of which dares to claim that they have it right.

---

1. W. B. Yeats, "The Second Coming," in *The Collected Poems of W. B. Yeats*, ed.
Richard J. Finneran (New York: Scribner, 1996), p. 187.

The Article by which the Church Stands or Falls

The church of Jesus Christ throughout the ages has clung to a center that prevails against every tide that would tear it asunder. That center is Jesus Christ himself. Jesus Christ is for the church not a mere artifact from the ancient world, not a proof text from the sacred page, not an orthodox christological formula. Jesus Christ is a living person. Jesus Christ—the one who was born in a stable, instantiated the reign of God, healed the sick, died on the cross, and was raised from the dead—continues to meet us as today. Jesus Christ encounters us in Word and Sacrament. In the proclaimed Word of a sermon, the sung Word of a hymn, the taught Word from the Bible, and the consoling Word of a sister or brother in Christ, Jesus Christ is present. In the water of Baptism, Jesus Christ unites the baptized to his own crucified and risen existence. In the bread and wine of the Holy Communion, Jesus Christ is present to give us his own body and blood, efficacious for the forgiveness of our sins. Jesus Christ is as alive today as ever before in human history. Wherever Jesus Christ is present, there the gospel occurs.

Jesus Christ is the center, without whom the church falls apart. Everything else depends on us, who are the church, staying connected to the one who is the center. How is this possible? John Calvin sardonically observed that human nature is "a perpetual factory of idols." [2] Every moment of our lives, we are tempted to turn away from the one who is the source of all life and find instead another center. If at its core the postmodern is defined by the absence of meta-narratives that serve to bind social existence together,[3] the naked public square soon becomes saturated with a cacophony of voices, each claiming a version of truth. Who can arbitrate the confusion of this Babel?

---

2. John Calvin, *Institutes of the Christian Religion*, ed. John T. McNeill, trans. Ford Lewis Battles (Philadelphia: Westminster, 1960), p. 108 (1.11.8).

3. Cf. Jean-Francois Lyotard, *The Postmodern Condition: A Report of Knowledge*, trans. Geoff Bennington and Brian Massumi (Minneapolis: University of Minnesota, 1993), pp. 39-41.

Within the Lutheran tradition, one final communal standard has been embedded as a strategy for countering our propensity for idolatry: the doctrine of justification. *The Smalcald Articles* assert this bold declaration about justification: "On this article stands all that we teach and practice." [4] Martin Luther expounded the article thus: Here is the first and chief article:

That Jesus Christ, our God and Lord, "was handed over to death for our trespasses and was raised for our justification" (Rom. 4[:25]); and he alone is "the Lamb of God, who takes away the sin of the world" (John 1[:29]); and "the Lord has laid on him the iniquity of us all" (Isa. 53[:6]); furthermore, "All have sinned," and "they are now justified without merit by his grace, through the redemption that is in Christ Jesus . . . by his blood" (Rom. 3[:23-25]). [5]

In the succinct formula of Article 5 of the Augsburg Confession, "we receive forgiveness of sin and become righteous before God out of grace for Christ's sake through faith." [6] The doctrine of justification also holds prominent place in other Christian traditions. The *Joint Declaration on the Doctrine of Justification* issued by the Lutheran World Federation and the Roman Catholic Church sets forth this common understanding of justification:

By grace alone, in faith in Christ's saving work and not because of any merit on our part, we are accepted by God and receive the Holy Spirit, who renews our hearts while equipping and calling us to good works. [7]

What does this mean? The doctrine of justification operates as a regulator that insists on the centrality of Jesus Christ and defends

---

4. *The Smalcald Articles*, in *The Book of Concord: The Confessions of the Evangelical Lutheran Church*, ed. Robert Kolb and Timothy J. Wengert (Minneapolis: Fortress, 2000), p. 301 (5).

5. Ibid., p. 301 (1-3).

6. The Augsburg Confession, in *The Book of Concord*, pp. 38, 40 (1).

7. *The Joint Declaration on Justification* (Grand Rapids: Eerdmans, 2000), p. 15 (15).

the integrity of the gospel that Jesus Christ brings. To advocate that salvation occurs by grace *alone* through faith *alone* in Christ *alone* gives the church a compass so that we might carefully adhere to the center, without which nothing else knows its correct location. What Jesus Christ brings is the gospel: pure, undefiled, exquisite gospel. As a gift from God, we receive the death and resurrection of Jesus Christ. As a gift, we receive baptism into this death and resurrection. As a gift, we receive the forgiveness of our sins. As a gift, we receive the body and blood of Jesus Christ in Holy Communion. As a gift, we are delivered from the power of the devil. As a gift, we receive the fruits of the Spirit, including love, joy, peace, patience, and kindness (cf. Galatians 5:22-23). As a gift, we receive eternal life. The doctrine of justification preserves the gospel-character of the gospel of Jesus Christ.

The Lutheran confessional stance advocates that the gospel of Jesus Christ, grounded in his death and resurrection, is the center that holds together the entire Christian faith. In every age, our time included, there are a multitude of contenders that would supplant the center. Let me make reference to two of my favorite ideas, the notions of "self-differentiated leadership" and "non-anxious presence" from family systems theory.[8] I am of the mind that one of the most helpful ideas for church leaders today is the concept of non-anxious presence as the basis for giving self-differentiated leadership. The goal of self-differentiated leadership is twofold. On the one hand, one needs to remain "connected" to the people one serves, demonstrating genuine and deep care for them. On the other hand, one must exert the freedom to take non-reactive positions on the issues and threats confronting the system. This entails the willingness to say, "This is how I see it," regardless of what others might think, while allowing others also to state their views. It sounds like a simple formula: "Love people genuinely; let people know what you think." The key to being able to lead in this way is based on what Edwin Friedman calls "non-anxious presence." If at

---

8. Cf. Edwin H. Friedman, *Generation to Generation: Family Process in Church and Synagogue* (New York: Guilford, 1985), pp. 103f. and 228-230.

the core of your own being you have the equanimity to lead in this way, you will do well.

The following question inevitably arises: "How do I become non-anxious?" This is an especially important question in giving leadership around controversial issues in the church. Moreover, this question is inadequately answered in family systems theory. In part, one moves toward becoming non-anxious by understanding one's own family of origin, how one tends to react based on the most formative relationships of one's own childhood. Never, however, can one become fully non-anxious through therapy or self-knowledge. If one is to live a non-anxious life, I contend it is only by the power of the gospel. It is only by the grace of God through faith in Jesus Christ. I trust in what God has done for me in Jesus Christ and receive freedom for living, including freedom to exemplify self-differentiated leadership. In this way the doctrine of justification is not only a theological construct designed to define, defend, and preserve the center of the Christian faith, it is also the central article necessary for my own existential existence as a fearful human being. The doctrine of justification is not only the article by which the church stands or falls, it is that article by which my own life stands or falls.

The Center under Attack

Quarrels and division have threatened to destroy the church at other times in history. While the issues that threaten to divide and tear us apart today are very real, we need to gain perspective on present conflicts by attending to the wisdom of those who have gone before us. The New Testament offers us testimony from one of the most fractious churches of all time, the church in Corinth. Consider some of the issues that Paul addresses in 1 Corinthians that were matters of contention: incest, lawsuits brought before unbelievers, sexuality, immorality, celibacy, eating meat sacrificed to idols, divisions at the Lord 's Table, competition regarding spiritual gifts, the proper exercise of the gift of tongues, whether the dead are raised, and the nature of the resurrection body. Underlying all these issues was the reality of a church deeply divided into rival factions, especially between rich and poor. It appears as though some were claiming a position of superiority over others based on the measure of the Spirit they possessed in comparison to others.

How does one begin to respond as a leader to a church facing deep controversy? Before we make reference to Paul's advice about any of the particular matters under discussion, it is vital that we first acknowledge the framework he constructs within which the entire debate will take place. That framework is found in the first chapter of 1 Corinthians. Clearly in Corinth, to employ the imagery of Yeats, the center was not holding. Paul makes an appeal to the congregation "that all of you be in agreement and that there be no divisions among you, but that you be united in the same mind and the same purpose" (1:10). The following verses make reference to quarrels and to contesting factions in the church. But Paul does not immediately enter into debate about any of the divisive issues. He does something far more important. He points the Corinthians to that which takes priority over all other matters. He reminds them of that which is truly the center of the faith, the cross of Christ:

> God chose what is low and despised in the world, things that are not, to reduce to nothing things that are, so that no one might boast in the presence of God. He is the source of your life in Christ Jesus, who became for us wisdom from God, and righteousness and sanctification and redemption, in order that, as it is written, "Let the one who boasts, boast in the Lord."
>
> — 1 Corinthians 1:28-31, NRSV

Paul proclaims that Jesus Christ is the center of the faith that can hold the church together, even in the midst of sharp differences. Only by negotiating the way through our differences by professing the centrality of Christ crucified might the church be able to hold together in the face of what threatens to cause disintegration.

Paul's logic at the start of the letter to the Corinthians is exactly the same as the logic of the Lutheran confessions regarding the doctrine of justification. Jesus Christ, the crucified and resurrected, is the only center that can prevent us from consuming each other. Moreover, the gospel of the crucified and risen Jesus Christ is the source of our unity and mission as his followers. Jesus Christ makes us into one body (12:12f.). All of the parts of the body are to function together for the common good. And Jesus Christ creates us to be a people in mission: "Therefore, my beloved, be steadfast, immovable, always excelling in the work of the Lord, because you know that in the Lord your labor is not in vain" (15:58).

Justification: Center of Our Unity and Mission

The unity of the church is not something we create. To think that the unity of the church depends on our actions is one of the most pervasive fallacies about the ecumenical movement. The unity of the church is a gift. To be more precise, the unity of the church is a gift of the gospel of Jesus Christ. By faith in the gospel of Jesus Christ, I am crucified in my sinful alienation from God and I am resurrected into new life in Christ. This identification with the person of Jesus Christ is the common experience of every Christian believer. "I have been crucified with Christ; and it is no longer I who live, but it is Christ who lives in me. And the life I now live in the flesh I live by faith in the Son of God, who loved me and gave himself for me" (Galatians 2:19-20). The event of justification, by which Christians become united with the death and resurrection of Christ, is the basis for the church's unity.

Because each of us is united with the death and resurrection of Jesus Christ, those who are Christians share this new crucified/risen identity in common. Each of us has been joined to the person of Jesus Christ. Jesus Christ is the one who holds us together with one another. Employing the imagery of 1 Corinthians 12, the body of Christ is singular. There is only one body of Christ. Yet each of us, through the event of justification, has been united to this one body. Each of us is a member of the one body of Jesus Christ by virtue of our incorporation into his death and resurrection.

> For just as the body is one and has many members, and all the members of the body, though many, are one body, so it is with Christ. For in the one Spirit we were all baptized into one body—Jews or Greeks, slaves or free—and we were all made to drink of one Spirit.
>
> — 1 Corinthians 12:12-13, NRSV

This act of being united to Jesus Christ occurs to each of us by virtue of our being justified in Christ. The unity of the church thus occurs as a gift, a gift based on our justification. Because we are joined to the death and resurrection of the one Jesus Christ, we are also joined to each other in one church. Justification in the gospel, the center of Christian existence, is the basis of our unity. Unity is not something we can create. God in Jesus Christ has already made us one. All we can do is destroy the gift God has already entrusted to us.

Similarly, the mission of the gospel is not something *we* do. To think otherwise is again a fundamental theological mistake. Too often we assume that mission is our human response to what God has done for us: "God saves; we do mission." This view fails to recognize, however, that God is the missionary, and we participate in God's mission. God's work in sending Jesus Christ into the world is God's own missionary endeavor. The joining of sinners to the death of Christ and the justification of sinners that makes them new creatures in Christ is God's quintessential mission work.

The triune God is a missionary God.[9] The primary means that God employs in mission is the gospel that is mediated through the preaching of the Word and participation in the Sacraments. When the church gathers around Word and Sacrament, the primary actor in the drama of worship is our missionary God. The event of my believing in the gospel—being joined to the death of Christ, and my being recreated in the image of Christ—belongs entirely to the *missio Dei*. As I am justified in Christ, I become a member of the one body of Christ, united to all other believers who themselves have been joined to the death and resurrection of Jesus Christ. The members of the one body of Christ are taken up into the mission of God by the power of the Holy Spirit. It is not that I or we *do* mission. It is far more accurate to say that by the

---

9. Cf. Craig L. Nessan, "Missionary God; Missionary Congregations," *Dialog* 40 (Summer 2001):112–117.

power of God at work in our lives in Christ, we become participants in the mission that God is bringing about through the church for the world.

The divine mission is to take up all flesh into its compass for the accomplishment of the kingdom of God.

Then comes the end, when he hands over the kingdom of God the Father, after he has destroyed every ruler and every authority and power. For he must reign until he has put all his enemies under his feet. The last enemy to be destroyed is death. For "God has put all things in subjection under his feet." When all things are subjected to him, then the Son himself will also be subjected to the one who put all things in subjection under him, so that God may be all in all.

° ⟵ 1 Corinthians 15:24-28, NRSV

The triune God engages in an eschatological mission that has as its alpha point the justification of the sinner and its omega point the restoration of all goodness in the kingdom of God. The driving force of this divine mission is the power of the Holy Spirit.

It is crucial to understand how justification is not merely the presupposition for the unity and mission of the church. Something far more radical is the case. Justification is the center that creates the unity of the church and mediates God's mission in and through the church. Unity and mission are given in, with, and under the gospel of Jesus Christ. This means that there is no controversial issue that can negate the unity and the mission of the church. If justification, as the article upon which the church stands or falls, holds as the center, then the unity and mission of the church are sustained. If justification, however, no longer holds as the true center of the church's life, then the unity and mission of the church have also been sacrificed. Everything depends on whether justification by grace through faith in Jesus Christ alone suffices as the center that holds the church together. The question we face in dealing with every controversial matter is this: "Can the center hold?"

The Ultimate and the Penultimate

The ELCA currently faces questions regarding whether the church should offer the blessing of committed same-gender relationships and allow the ordination/rostering of approved candidates in such relationships.

In deliberating issues as emotionally charged and divisive as these, it is essential that we be absolutely clear that justification is the central conviction of the church that holds us in unity and sends us in mission. All parties who engage in debates about controversial issues must first pledge themselves to hold the gospel of justification as their chief and highest commitment, if the center is to hold against the tides of opinion that threaten to tear us apart.

It is no small matter to have full clarity about what makes us into and binds us together as members of the one church. We are not required to have unanimity about every ethical question. Bracketing out for the moment the possibility that Scripture excludes certain options from consideration, the freedom of the gospel generally allows for a range of viewpoints on challenging ethical issues. What we insist upon is prior agreement that we are all saved by grace through faith in Jesus Christ alone. This doctrinal affirmation provides the framework within which all serious discussion of contested matters must take place. The doctrine of justification provides the focal point of the Christian faith. When we each confess our own sinfulness and need for the forgiveness that Jesus Christ offers as a gift, the foundation is laid by which we may engage one another in humility concerning matters about which we take strong positions.

In his book *Ethics*, Dietrich Bonhoeffer makes a vital distinction between the "ultimate" and the "penultimate" that contributes greatly to our proper engagement in debates about ethical issues. By the ultimate Bonhoeffer means what God has accomplished by working the justification of the sinner. The ultimate anchors Christian existence in God's mercy toward sinners as the final word about human existence. The ultimate provides the point of orientation—the center, for all the rest of the Christian life.

The word of the justifying grace of God never departs from its position as the final word; it never yields itself simply as a result that has been achieved, a result that might just as well be set at the beginning as at the end. The way from the penultimate to the ultimate can never be dispensed with.[10]

The penultimate, by contrast, always defers to the priority of justification as God's ultimate activity. The penultimate "is everything that precedes the ultimate, everything that precedes the justification of the sinner by grace alone, everything which is to be regarded as leading up to the last thing when the last thing has been found."[11] This does not mean the penultimate is unimportant. On the contrary, penultimate concerns are of urgent importance. We live most of our lives with regard for penultimate issues that warrant our serious attention and highest quality reflection. These involve matters that contribute greatly to the welfare of other persons and the integrity of God's creation. We are called to give careful and wise consideration to a host of penultimate issues, including the church's best thought in deliberating ethical questions about human sexuality. A clear definition of the ultimate does mean, however, that penultimate matters finally must yield to the ultimate as the center of the church's faith, unity, and mission. What we decide about penultimate issues has deep and profound effects on ourselves and on the lives of others. The decisions made about penultimate matters have many ramifications for the shape of the church's mission. But finally these must never supplant the justification of the sinner by grace through faith in Jesus Christ alone as God's final word!

Here is one crucial implication of maintaining a clear distinction between justification as God's ultimate word and ethical decisions as penultimate concerns: We must avoid aligning any particular position in the homosexuality debate with the gospel itself. The gospel is God's act of forgiving sinners by grace in Jesus Christ.

---

10. Dietrich Bonhoeffer, *Ethics*, ed. Eberhard Bethge, trans. Neville Horton Smith (New York: Macmillan, 1955), p. 83.

11. Ibid., p. 91.

This is God's unconditional act of mercy, a gift to sinners regardless of how adequately they think about any particular question facing the church. Whenever we enter into the discussion of controversial issues, however, we experience the temptation of claiming our own position as that view that corresponds with God's own viewpoint. I am tempted to confuse my own conclusion on a particular issue with the gospel itself. I want to identify what I think with God's gospel truth.

Neither the view that the church should bless committed same-gender relationships nor the view that the church should refuse to bless committed same-gender relationships should be identified with the gospel of justification by grace through faith in Jesus Christ alone. Neither the refusal to ordain/roster persons in committed same-gender relationships nor the decision to ordain/roster persons in committed same-gender relationships is *the* gospel position. How one thinks about these questions, important as they are for the well-being of many, must not become a litmus test for determining one's faithfulness to the gospel of Jesus Christ. The gospel is that message by which people on every side of the discussion are each justified by grace and forgiven for Christ's sake. The unity of the church and faithfulness to God's mission depend on our keeping clear the distinction between ultimate and penultimate with reference to the study of homosexuality in which the church has been engaging. In classical Lutheran terms, to identify any ethical position on a particular issue with the gospel itself is to fail to properly distinguish between law and gospel.

If we, as members of the church entrusted with the gospel in this generation, are able to honor justification by grace through faith in Jesus Christ alone as the center of our church, we will be able to engage in the conversation about homosexuality in humility, listening to those with whom we disagree and seeking faithfulness in our own views. If we look into the face of our neighbor, no matter how she or he thinks about committed same-gender relationships, and see a sister or brother for whom Christ died, then we will be able to weather even this intensely emotional discussion.

Questions for Reflection

For personal reflection

1. Do you have any anxiety as you begin reading a book about homosexuality and the church? What are the reasons for these feelings?

2. How does your faith in Jesus Christ help you relate to people with whom you disagree?

For group discussion

1. What are some of the issues in the past that could have torn apart the Lutheran church?

2. How does our faith in God's grace and forgiveness in Jesus Christ hold the church together when we deal with controversial issues?

3. If justification by grace through faith in Jesus Christ is our only "ultimate," what does the author mean by saying we should keep ethical issues "penultimate"?

My Life Flows On in Endless Song

With One Voice # 781

My life flows on in endless song;
above earth's lamentation,
I catch the sweet, though far-off hymn
that hails a new creation.

Refrain
No storm can shake my inmost calm
while to that Rock I'm clinging.
Since Christ is Lord of heaven and earth,
how can I keep from singing?

Through all the tumult and the strife,
I hear that music ringing.
It finds an echo in my soul.
How can I keep from singing?

Refrain

What though my joys and comforts die?
The Lord my Savior liveth.
What though the darkness gather round?
Songs in the night he giveth.

Refrain

The peace of Christ makes fresh my heart,
a fountain ever springing!
All things are mine since I am his!
How can I keep from singing?

Refrain

Text: Robert Lowry, 1826-1899.

2

The Root of
the Present Impasse

Two Irreconcilable Hermeneutics

What divides the church regarding matters of homosexuality is deep and intractable. Sexuality, which the Christian tradition holds as a great gift of God, is still very much a mystery. What was God thinking to instill deep within us attractions and desires that draw us toward other persons with such overwhelming power? If I am honest in the examination of my own life as a sexual being, there is much that is unfathomable to me. There are fears and impulses that can feel threatening and overwhelming.

One of the chief responsibilities of the church is to articulate a sexual ethic that is faithful to the tradition in ordering our lives together as sexual beings. Yet the nature of our sexual existence is such that it is very difficult for us as a church to hold constructive conversations on the topic. To speak of human sexuality is to discuss an aspect of human existence that is deeply rooted in what we hold very personal and precious. My beliefs and my emotions are greatly invested in a certain way of ordering sexual morality. When my own deep convictions confront your own deep convictions, this is a recipe for a clash of views.

If it is difficult for us as a church to hold constructive conversation on the topic of sexuality in general, the questions surrounding homosexuality are even more complicated to unravel. What does the Bible have to say about homosexuality? How should the church relate to self-identified homosexual persons? How should a congregation minister to homosexual persons who are members of the church, and the families of these people? How should the church deal with the candidacy of homosexual persons preparing for public and rostered ministry in the church? Then there are the two questions under study by the ELCA:

1 Should the church bless committed same-gender relationships?

2. Should the church roster (in the case of pastoral ministry, ordain) approved candidates who are in committed same-gender relationships?

We are all aware of how polarized the views on these questions and how strident the voices contending for various positions. One of my own convictions surrounding the decisions facing our church is that this topic involves more than two positions, pro or con. Rather, there exists a full spectrum of views on any one of the questions already cited. Our discussion easily becomes sidetracked because we are quick to label a particular viewpoint according to a rhetoric of polarization, assigning it to one of the two caricatured options. Our public conversation will be enhanced when we intentionally represent a range of views, paying attention to nuances of opinion, rather than structuring every debate as though there were only two mutually exclusive positions.

In fact, one of the chief obstacles to negotiating a way through the present impasse is the reduction of every debate to a contest between two incompatible ways of construing the evidence. Before offering my own proposal for a middle path, I will set forth an analysis of the current debate, arguing that the current structure of the discussion regarding the use of biblical and scientific arguments only deepens the impasse. The problem is deepened by the competition between two mutually contradictory hermeneutics for interpreting the contested biblical texts, as well as two equally divisive approaches to interpreting the scientific evidence.

Two Irreconcilable Hermeneutics

Probably the most irreconcilable aspect of the debate over homosexuality is its reduction to a contest between two contradictory ways of interpreting the seven biblical texts most often cited as definitive for an appraisal of how the church should deal with homosexuals: Genesis 19:1-29; Leviticus 18:22; Leviticus 20:13; Judges 19; Romans 1:26-27; 1 Corinthians 6:9; and 1 Timothy 1:10. Across the church it has been typical to begin a conversation about homosexuality and Christian faith by examining these particular passages. Because we are a church that is grounded in a commitment to "the canonical Scriptures as the authoritative source and norm for its proclamation, faith, and life," we turn to the Bible in order to negotiate matters of ethical concern in our lives.[12] Frequently, our procedure for investigating these texts has entailed some form of debate between advocates of two diametrically opposed ways of interpreting these texts. In the following paragraphs I will sketch the shape of the two sets of arguments that emerge employing this approach.

I will call this first hermeneutic the *traditional* approach. Two recent scholars who are representative of the traditional approach are Robert A. J. Gagnon[13] and Richard B. Hays.[14] I will especially draw on their research in describing this hermeneutic. A major presupposition guiding this interpretation of the contested texts involves a deep conviction about the natural order created by God. In the beginning, God created human beings, male and female (cf. Genesis 1:26-27). There exists in creation what Gagnon calls "gender complementarity." This complementarity is evidenced in human anatomy, how man and woman fit together in the act of having sexual relations. While not the only purpose of sexual relations, the joining of male sperm with the female ovum for procreation is basic to the natural order of creation. "Be fruitful and multiply" (Genesis 1:28). Homosexual relations contradict this

---

12. Constitution of the Evangelical Lutheran Church in America, 2.03.

13. Robert A. J. Gagnon, *The Bible and Homosexual Practice: Texts and Hermeneutics* (Nashville: Abingdon, 2001). It is significant that Gagnon chooses "homosexual practice" in the title of his book. He understands that the concept of "sexual orientation" is irrelevant to an interpretation of the biblical authors.

14. Richard B. Hays, *The Moral Vision of the New Testament: A Contemporary Introduction to New Testament Ethics* (San Francisco: HarperSanFrancisco, 1996), especially chapter 16.

natural order, ignoring the gender complementarity created by God and eliminating the possibility of procreation. According to this traditional approach, the strong aversion many people experience in thinking about homosexual relations indicates further how this natural order is established in the human psyche.

This major presupposition about the created structure of the natural order provides the overarching framework for interpreting the seven debated passages. Leviticus 18:22 and 20:13 belong to the holiness code of the Old Testament. "You shall not lie with a male as with a woman; it is an abomination" (Leviticus 18:22). Leviticus 20:13 adds the punishment for this offense, stating that "they shall be put to death; their blood be upon us." This consequence is consistent with the penalty for other major violations of the Holiness Code. Gagnon's summary reasoning for this legal provision relates directly to its contradicting the natural order created by God:

> Hence, the most likely reason why homosexual intercourse was viewed as wrong in Lev 18:22 and 20:13 was that it mixed two partners in sexual intercourse that God the Creator never intended to be joined: two males. For one man to "lie with" another man in the manner that men normally "lie with" a woman was to defile the latter's masculine stamp, impressed by God and evident in both the visible sexual complementarity of male and female and in the sacred lore of creation. The very integrity and health of the family unit was also undermined. Inability to procreate and misuse of semen were important secondary factors. [15]

Hays underscores how this "unambiguous legal prohibition stands as the foundation for the subsequent universal rejection of male same-sex intercourse within Judaism." [16]

Genesis 19:1-29 records the story of the destruction of Sodom and Gomorrah, while Judges 19:10-30 describes a parallel case of wickedness at Gibeah. Both stories describe how men demand that the male guest(s) be handed over to them so that they may have

---

15. Gagnon, p. 142. Cf. Hays, p. 386.
16. Hays, p. 381.

intercourse with them/him. In both instances, the host offers women (daughters/concubine) from within the house instead. Both stories conclude with severe punishment against the cities where such horrible sin was perpetrated. In the case of Sodom, the punishment was the utter destruction of the city and its inhabitants. In the case of Gibeah, the Israelites wreaked vengeance on the tribe of Benjamin for its defense of the crime. Traditionally, the "sin" of Sodom and Gomorrah came to be identified with homosexuality. Thus the definition of *sodomy* is "copulation with a member of the same sex."

In his book, Hays does not even discuss Judges 19 and dismisses Genesis 19 as "irrelevant to the topic."[17] Gagnon, on the other hand, holds that both of these texts resonate with the traditional condemnation of homosexual behavior. While Gagnon grants that the sins of inhospitality and rape magnify the wickedness of those who committed these acts, this does not mitigate that the demand for homosexual relations is also a serious cause for offense. "A strict either-or interpretation, *either* homosexual/bisexual lust *or* an aggressive disgrace of visitors, goes beyond the wording of the text and imposes a distinction that did not always hold true in the ancient world."[18] The threat of homosexual intercourse only increases the horror regarding the severity of the sin.

Supporters of the traditional view argue that Romans 1:26-27 is the most significant New Testament passage that makes direct reference to homosexual acts. In Romans, Paul argues that fundamental knowledge about the sovereignty of God can be known through the creation. God's "eternal power and divine nature, invisible though they are, have been understood and seen through the things he has made" (Romans 1:20). It is because of humankind's rejection of this natural knowledge of God that they have "exchanged the glory of the immortal God for images resembling a mortal human being or birds or four-footed animals or reptiles" (Romans 1:23). As a result of human idolatry, "God gave them up in the lusts of their hearts to

---

17. Ibid., p. 381.
18. Gagnon, p. 77.

impurity, to the degrading of their bodies" (Romans 1:24). Paul goes on to write in verses 26-27:

> For this reason God gave them up to degrading passions. Their women exchanged natural intercourse for unnatural, and in the same way also the men, giving up natural intercourse with women, were consumed with passion for one another. Men committed shameless acts with men and received in their own persons the due penalty for their error.
>
> — Romans 1:26-27, NRSV

In these verses, homosexual behavior is offered as a dramatic example of the degree to which human idolatry leads to moral depravity. The reference to "natural intercourse" and "unnatural" illustrates how Paul based his argument on the understanding of the natural order given by God at the creation of the world.

Paul's general argument in the first chapters of Romans aims to demonstrate how neither Jews nor pagans have any excuse when standing before the face of God, stating that "all have sinned and fall short of the glory of God" (Romans 3:23). The reference to homosexual intercourse is offered in Romans 1 as a sordid example of the consequences of the human rejection of God for idols. Paul assumes that this evidence will be self-explanatory in convincing the reader of the sins of the Gentile world. The implication is that the practice of homosexual intercourse in the pagan world would be well-known and assumed to be worthy of condemnation.

Romans 1:26-27 is interpreted to resonate with, reinforce, and even expand the Old Testament's well-established rejection of homosexual behavior. This text expands the biblical view because it is the only reference to homosexual relations between women. Paul's appeal to the natural knowledge of God in the creation and to "natural intercourse" establishes his argument that sexual relations between male and female follows God's natural order. Same-sex intercourse, on the other hand, is "contrary to nature." Following Gagnon, "Paul in effect argues that even pagans who have no access to the book of Leviticus should know that same-sex eroticism is 'contrary to nature' because the primary sex organs fit male to female, not female to female or male to male." [19] Romans 1:26-27 are the most important New Testament verses that are cited to support of the traditional interpretation condemning homosexual relations. 1 Corinthians 6:9 and 1 Timothy 1:10 each consists of lists of sinners that include "sodomites," the term used in the New Revised Standard Version translation of the Bible. In 1 Corinthians 6:9, "male prostitutes" and "sodomites" are among those who will not inherit God's kingdom. In 1 Timothy 1:10, "sodomites" are listed among those who need the dictates of the law.

The two Greek words that have been translated as referring to homosexual behavior are *malakoi* ("male prostitutes" in the New Revised Standard Version of the Bible) and *arsenokoitai* ("sodomites" in NRSV). Gagnon argues that *malakoi*, with its literal meaning of "soft," refers to "males playing the female role in sexual intercourse with other males." [20] In place of the NRSV translation of *malakoi* as "male prostitutes," Gagnon would render the term as "effeminate males who play the sexual role of females." In both 1 Corinthians 6:9 and 1 Timothy 1:10, Gagnon holds that the word *arsenokoitai* means "males who take other males to bed." [21] Gagnon defends this usage of the words with reference to non-biblical texts from the period. [22] Both Hays and Gagnon contend that these words, particularly *arsenokoitai*, are consistent with the condemnations against homosexual activity set forth in Leviticus. "Paul's use of the term [*arsenokoitai*] presupposes and reaffirms the holiness code's condemnation of homosexual acts." [23]

In addition to interpreting the biblical texts usually cited in the homosexuality debate, Gagnon further argues that Jesus endorses the understanding of the natural order of creation set forth in Genesis. Gagnon writes, "What is clear from the evidence that the texts do offer is that the historical Jesus is no defender of homosexual

---

19. Gagnon, p. 254.
20. Ibid., p. 308.
21. Ibid., pp. 308f.
22. Ibid., pp. 309-312, 317-322.
23. Hays, p. 382.

behavior. To the contrary, Jesus, both in what he says and what he fails to say, remains squarely on the side of those who reject homosexual practice."[24] The guiding presupposition of the traditional approach to interpreting the various biblical texts is valid also for Jesus. The natural order created by God, establishing the complementarity of male and female, is decisive for the proper interpretation of both Old and New Testaments, including the Jesus tradition.

I will call the the second hermeneutic the *contextual* approach. Two scholars who are representative of this viewpoint are Robin Scroggs[25] and Martti Nissinen.[26] Like the traditional approach, this approach too is significantly shaped by a major presupposition. Here, the guiding presupposition is that none of the debated biblical texts has as the object of its concern the type of homosexual relationship currently under consideration by the church. People living in the ancient world did not have a concept of sexual orientation as a factor that conditions sexual attraction. Ancient people also did not have the concept of a committed same-gender relationship between two consenting adults. Within this contextual view, it would be anachronistic to expect biblical authors to refer to the type of homosexual relationship that has only begun to emerge in the modern world. For this reason, the various texts cited by authors of the traditional approach have limited validity when discussing homosexuality, because none of these passages has in its purview a committed and lifelong relationship between two adults of same-gender orientation.

With regard to the two texts from the Holiness Code, Leviticus 18:22 and 20:13, Nissinen argues that these prohibitions against a man lying "with a male as with a woman" are frequently interpreted as being directed against the Israelites taking up cultic practices of the Canaanites. When Leviticus 20:13 calls such behavior an "abomination," this is consistent with other texts that prohibit practices associated with the worship of foreign gods or

24. Gagnon, p. 228.

25. Robin Scroggs, *The New Testament and Homosexuality* (Philadelphia: Fortress, 1983).

26. Martti Nissinen, *Homoeroticism in the Biblical World: A Historical Perspective*, trans. Kirsi Stjerna (Minneapolis: Fortress, 1998), p. 39.

idols. This would mean that the type of homosexual intercourse addressed by these two texts is "sacred prostitution" within the context of a "fertility cult." [27] While partially valid, Nissinen finds this interpretation too limited in scope, however. A larger concern of the Leviticus texts has to do with the prescribing of gender roles within the patriarchal order of ancient society. This leads to his threefold conclusion:

1. The prohibition of sexual contact between males in the Holiness Code in Leviticus 18:22 and 20:13 is done in a context of a polemic against a non-Israelite cult. Because the records of cultic homoeroticism are scanty and not unequivocal, however, historical description of this context is difficult.

2. The strategy of postexilic Israelites to maintain their distinct identity by, among other ways, separating from others strengthened the already existing taboos and social standards regarding sexual behavior and gender roles, banning, for instance, castration, cross-dressing, and male same-sex behavior.

3. Israel shared with its cultural environment an understanding of sexual life as an interaction between active masculine and passive feminine gender roles. This interaction was the cornerstone of gender identity, but the concept of sexual orientation was unknown. Sexual contact between two men was prohibited because the passive party assumed the role of a woman and his manly honor was thus disgraced. [28]

Each of these three factors conditions the interpretation of the Leviticus texts and limits their relevance for the current conversation about committed same-gender relationships.

According to the contextual hermeneutic, Genesis 19:1-29 and Judges 19 have virtually nothing to do with the current conversation about homosexuality. The central theme of both texts involves an extreme breech of the practice of hospitality, valued so highly in

---

27. Ibid., p. 39
28. Ibid., p. 44.

Israelite culture. Nissinen writes, "In the Jesus tradition the sin of Sodom is an example of the lack of hospitality."[29] In this situation, the men of the city are intent on subjecting the visitors to violent homosexual rape. Whereas the conventional definition of sodomy refers to anal intercourse between two men, a more accurate reading would identify the sins of Sodom (and Gibeah) as pride, inhospitality, xenophobia, violence, and rape. This is gang rape aimed at disgracing manly honor—humiliation, subjugation, and domination. Finally, there is very little of positive value for the deliberation of sexual ethics in these texts. At most they provide a glaring condemnation of rape, including same-sex rape.

In discussing the New Testament texts most cited in the debate over homosexuality, both Nissinen and Scroggs devote significant attention to the practice of pederasty in classical antiquity. Scroggs argues that the primary form of homosexual relationship in the Greco-Roman world involved pederastic friendship, a relationship between an older male who was responsible for the education and cultivation of a younger male.[30] In that male-dominated society, the ideal form of beauty was the beautiful boy. The pederastic friendship lasted over a period of years, from the time of puberty until the younger male reached maturity around age 20. One of the basic characteristics of pederasty was the development of homosexual relations between the older and younger male. Scroggs criticizes the practice of pederasty for the inequality, impermanence, and potential humiliation in the relationship. After examining the ancient arguments that were set forth in favor of and against pederasty, Scroggs concludes:

> From our perspective the practices of pederasty in the ancient world do raise serious moral questions, questions of denigration and dehumanization of the boys—issues that were discussed in the debate [of the time]. Yet I do not sense any *homophobia* in the texts under discussion, although there is plenty of *misogyny*.[31]

---

29. Ibid., p. 47.
30. Cf. for the following, Scroggs, pp. 17-65.
31. Ibid., p. 62.

Palestinian Judaism reacted strongly against the practice of pederasty in the surrounding culture.[32] Hellenistic Judaism further vilified the ideal of pederastic friendship. The examination of the evidence leads Scroggs to conclude that the "homosexuality the New Testament opposes is the pederasty of the Greco-Roman culture; the attitudes toward pederasty and, in part, the language used to oppose it are informed by the Jewish background."[33]

Nissinen updates this argument in his more recent book, examining additional texts from the ancient world. He adds further data about homoerotic prostitution, particularly about practices in the Roman world. As Nissinen states, prostitution, including male homosexual prostitution, was a common, legal, and tolerated occurrence in the Roman streets and baths.[34] The Romans, in contrast to the Greeks, did not uphold the pederastic ideal of pedagogy of a young man. Instead, homoerotic relationships exploited the power difference between superior and inferior. Morally, the disgrace in such a homoerotic relationship applied only to the inferior, passive partner.[35] Jewish writings of the period severely condemn both the pederastic practices and the exploitative homosexual prostitution of the time.

The contextual hermeneutic stresses how in Romans 1:26-27, Paul employs "same-sex sexual relations as an example of an indecent life precisely for the reason that they best rhetorically illustrate the exchanging of God for idols."[36] This example is offered as a contemporary practice that illustrated Paul's larger theological argument of the passage, that no one is without excuse when it comes to sin. Paul selects the egregious example of pederasty to demonstrate how the Gentile world is also captive to sin. Paul abides by the existing Jewish wisdom of the time in making this judgment. Nissinen adds the argument that when Romans 1:26-27 describes homosexual relations as "unnatural," this is with reference

---

32. Cf. ibid., pp. 66-98.
33. Ibid., p. 84.
34. Nissinen, p. 70.
35. Cf. ibid., pp. 69-73.
36. Ibid., p. 106.

to the established gender roles of the time and should not be universalized.[37] Nissinen discounts the possibility that Paul could have had any notion of concept of sexual orientation as it is understood today. Instead, Paul only was referring to the practice of certain existing forms of homoeroticism, specifically pederasty, prostitution, and other practices known to the congregation at Rome, including some between women. Paul's "statements cannot be understood as if they deal with 'homosexuality' theoretically and generally."[38]

According to Scroggs, the point of Romans 1-3 is to demonstrate the universality of the fall, with the concrete illustrations being secondary to the main argument.[39] Based on his extensive study of pederasty in the Greco-Roman world, Scroggs holds that the two terms listed in 1 Corinthians 6:9, *malakoi* and *arsenokoitai*, are both specific to the prevalent practice of pederasty. *Malakoi*, with its literal meaning of "soft" or "effeminate," refers to the younger male in a pederastic relationship, while *arsenokoitai* refers to the older male. To be more specific, Scroggs argues that a particularly exploitative form of pederasty is here condemned, that between an effeminate "call boy" and an older male who occasionally summons him for the purpose of sexual self-gratification.[40] The juxtaposition of *arsenokoites* with the word *andropodistes* (translated by Scroggs as "kidnapper" or "slave dealer") in 1 Timothy 1:10 leads him to the conclusion that this passage is targeting an even more destructive form of pederasty, "the enslaving of boys or youths for sexual purposes, and the use of these boys by male adults."[41]

Nissinen is more cautious than Scroggs in his assessment of 1 Corinthians 6:9 and 1 Timothy 1:10, and in defining the

---

37. Cf. for the following, Nissinen, pp. 106-113. David E. Fredrickson, "Natural and Unnatural Use in Romans 1:24-27: Paul and the Philosophic Critique of Eros," in David L. Balch, ed., *Homosexuality, Science, and the "Plain Sense" of Scripture* (Grand Rapids: Eerdmans, 2000), pp. 197-222, argues that what was understood to be "unnatural" was the excessive passion and loss of self-control that was demonstrated by these acts, not that they are same-sex relations.

38. Ibid., p. 113.

39. Scroggs, p. 114.

40. Scroggs, p. 108.

41. Ibid., pp. 120-121.

condemned behaviors as pederasty and enslavement To Nissinen, *malakoi* refers more generally to the effeminacy of one partner in a homosexual liaison; *arsenokoites* is even less clear. Nevertheless, Nissinen arrives at a conclusion that parallels that of Scroggs, that the "modern concept of 'homosexuality' should by no means be read into Paul's text. . . . What Paul primarily opposes is the wrong that people do to others." [42] Reading these biblical texts in their historical context severely limits their relevance for current debates about sexual orientation and committed same-gender partnerships. According to the contextual hermeneutic, just as historical interpretation of the Bible eventually led to a change in the institution of slavery or the role of women in the church (by allowing the ordination of women), so now the blessing of committed same-gender relationships may be warranted.

Assessment of the Arguments

Significant attention has been given to a sketch of the two sets of arguments most prominent in the debate over the place of homosexuality in the church. I have done so for three very important reasons.

First, it is extremely important to note how the fundamental presupposition taken at the outset determines the parameters of the interpretation and predetermines a particular conclusion. Regarding the traditional hermeneutic, the presupposition about the natural order of God's creation and gender complementarity guides the discussion of each of the individual texts. From the point of view of the contextual hermeneutic, the presupposition about the lack of a concept of sexual orientation in the ancient world and the vast cultural differences in the very definition of homosexuality, then and now, is decisive. One's guiding presupposition to the disputed texts conditions the exegetical conclusions that can be drawn.

Second, these two competing hermeneutics are irreconcilable with one another to the point of being mutually exclusive. I see no prospect

---

42. Nissinen, p. 118. Cf. Scroggs, p. 127: Biblical judgments against homosexuality are not relevant to today's debate.

for the emergence of a constructive proposal to the present impasse in the ELCA so long as the debate is framed as the choice between one of these two options. To continue the homosexuality debate as a contest between these two biblical positions is to create a situation in which there inevitably will be "winners" and "losers." This is a formula for schism within the church. For this reason I advocate that we intentionally start to frame the conversation as a continuum of many positions, rather than a choice between only these two extremes. This will require listening to voices—moderate voices—which have perhaps been silenced thus far in the conversation.

Third, having reflected on these two hermeneutics for many years, I have come to the conviction that the exegetical evidence warrants each of them. *Both of the prominent hermeneutical approaches have validity as being biblically based.* If one allows its guiding presupposition, the given position—either the traditional hermeneutic or the contextual one—has integrity and credibility. This, of course, makes the present impasse all the more impossible to resolve. We encounter in this debate the situation where two sets of arguments both are warranted with biblical authority.[43] This raises an acute ecclesiological question: Can the ELCA become catholic enough to encompass a spectrum of views on controversial social issues without resorting to the sectarian resolution of the tension through schism?

I want to add one more comment to this discussion of the two irreconcilable hermeneutics. Some have labored intensively for scientific evidence that might tip the scales in favor of either nature or nurture as the cause of homosexuality. Those who favor the full inclusion of homosexuals in the life of the church tend toward explanations that provide a genetic cause of homosexuality, thinking this will prove that sexual orientation is not something one chooses. Those who favor a clearly circumscribed role for homosexuals

---

43. I would argue that a similar dilemma emerged in the debate in the ELCA over the full communion agreement with the Episcopal Church, Called to Common Mission, only in that case the arguments were grounded in two incommensurate ways of appealing to the authority of the Lutheran Confessions.

in the church tend toward environmental explanations that attribute homosexuality to developmental factors, thinking this will prove that it is the world's sinfulness that leads someone to become homosexual. It is my observation that this debate also boils down to a contest between two irreconcilable hermeneutics. Taken to its logical extreme, this means that even if the proponents of a genetic explanation arrived at 100-percent proof that a certain gene sequence caused homosexual orientation, those who hold the opposite view could claim that this is the consequence of a defect in the genetic code, not God's creative intention. Again the guiding presupposition trumps the conclusion that is drawn. Again two irreconcilable hermeneutics attempt to seize the day.

Questions for Reflection

For personal reflection

1. How do you feel about discussing human sexuality with other people? Why do you feel that way?

2. What have you learned from this chapter about the way you interpret the Bible? What are your presuppositions when you read the passages about homosexuality?

For group discussion

1. What are the strengths of the traditional approach to interpreting what the Bible says about homosexuality?

2. What are the strengths of the contextual approach to interpreting what the Bible says about homosexuality?

3. How important is it that the members of the church are able to stay together in one church, even though they have different ways of interpreting the Bible? How do you think you could help them stay together?

Oh, Praise the Gracious Power

With One Voice # 750

Oh, praise the gracious power
that tumbles walls of fear
and gathers in one house of faith
all strangers far and near:

Refrain
We praise you, Christ! Your cross has made us one!

Oh, praise persistent truth
that opens fisted minds
and eases from their anxious clutch
the prejudice that blinds: *Refrain*

Oh, praise inclusive love,
encircling ev'ry race,
oblivious to gender, wealth,
to social rank or place: *Refrain*

Oh, praise the word of faith
that claims us as God's own,
a living temple built on Christ,
our rock and cornerstone: *Refrain*

Oh, praise the tide of grace
that laps at every shore
with visions of a world at peace,
no longer bled by war: *Refrain*

Oh, praise the power, the truth,
the love, the word, the tide.
Yet more than these, oh, praise their source,
praise Christ the crucified.   *Refrain*

Oh, praise the living Christ
with faith's bright songful voice!
Announce the Gospel to the world
and with these words rejoice: *Refrain*

3

Conflict of Interpretations

How Catholic Dare We Become?

There is one feature that all church conflicts have in common. Wherever division threatens the unity and wholeness of the church and wherever there are issues that are hotly contested, there we also discover radically different appeals to the authority of the faith. There we find conflicting interpretations of the meaning of Holy Scripture. Virtually every polarizing issue up for debate in the history of the church has been accompanied by competing hermeneutical principles and judgments.

Conflict at Corinth

In the Corinthian correspondence that we are especially referencing in these pages, we discover conflicting interpretations about God's will for the particular questions facing the congregation. At issue was the division of the community in the practice of eating the Lord's Supper, the question of eating meat that had been sacrificed to idols, the appeal on the part of Christians to Corinthian courts, speaking in tongues, the meaning of the resurrection of the dead, and conflict over certain sexual practices. In every case, Paul engages in theological argument with those who hold a dramatically different interpretation of the implications of the Christian faith.

In his book *The Corinthian Body*, Dale B. Martin examines the nature of that congregation's conflict in 1 Corinthians.[44] The reader's primary access to the views of Paul's opponents is embedded in the slogans Paul cites in order to refute them: "All things are lawful for me" (6:12); "Food is for the stomach and the stomach for food" (6:13); "It is well for a man not to touch a woman" (7:1); "all of us

---

44. Dale B. Martin, *The Corinthian Body* (New Haven: Yale, 1995).

possess knowledge" (8:1); "All things are lawful" (10:23); we might "speak in the tongues of mortals and of angels" (13:1); and "there is no resurrection of the dead" (15:12). Martin makes a compelling case that the conflict in the Corinthian church is between "the strong," a dominant minority within the congregation who were of high economic status, and "the weak," the majority of church members who were of lower economic status. The "higher status" Christians make appeals to special knowledge and special privileges that set them above the "lower status" Christians. The social hierarchy that gave them elite status according to the standards of the world is something they seek also to transfer over to their relationship to lower status Christians within the church.

The elite group brought a distinct presupposition to their participation in the church that was decisive for their engagement with the rest of the congregation. It was as if God was saying, "God has given us a privileged position in society. Because of our status, therefore we are free to eat what we want, therefore we are permitted sexual freedom, therefore we deserve priority at the Lord's Supper, therefore our gift of tongues is the greatest gift, therefore we transcend the resurrection of a dead corpse." Through a series of arguments, Paul challenges each of these claims to privilege by stressing the centrality of the cross of Christ and a non-hierarchical interpretation of the body of Christ. Notice how decisively the given presupposition shapes the elite interpretation of the Christian life.

Conflict of Interpretations

Which Abraham?

The kind of polemic at work at Corinth is not confined to the ancient world or to debates among Christians. This topic, in fact, is getting widespread attention in the mainstream media. The cover story of a recent issue of *Time* magazine reported on the contrasting ways each of the three great monotheistic faiths—Judaism, Christianity, and Islam—appeal to the tradition of Abraham.[45]

---

45. "The Legacy of Abraham," *Time*, September 30, 2002, pp. 64-75.

- For Jews, Abraham and Sarah are the ancestors who received the promise of a land, a nation of descendants, and God's special blessing (Genesis 12:1-3).

- For Christians, Abraham serves as an archetype for what it means to live by faith. Abraham is declared to be righteous by God, not because of the law nor by circumcision, but by faith in God's promise that has been fulfilled in Christ (Romans 4:13).

- For Muslims, Abraham is one of the four most important prophets of the faith, who serves as a central example of what it means to submit to the will of Allah. The Koran includes stories of Abraham that demonstrate his strong opposition to idols and his submission to God's will, even to the point of being ready to sacrifice his own son. That son, however, is Ishmael, not Isaac. This claim serves to reinforce the true genealogical line of Abraham, leading to the existence of the Muslims rather than the Jews.

The *Time* article raised the acute question of whether the three faiths can discover a basis for common ground in their shared ancestor, or whether the conflicting interpretations about Abraham can only lead to continued strife.

"Just war"?

Another contemporary issue that has divided Christians in their interpretation of Scripture and tradition has to do with the option for "just war" as an approach to resolving conflict in the world versus those who appeal to the Bible in support of non-violence.[46] The Hebrew Bible (Old Testament), in particular, provides precedent for God's people to engage in war in obedience to God's will. In the New Testament, the legitimizing of state authority occurs in passages such as Romans 13:1: "Let every person be subject to the

---

46. "For Peace in God's World," A Social Statement of the Evangelical Lutheran Church in America adopted on August 20, 1995, pp. 11-13.

governing authorities." Such a text lays the foundation for the later development of "just war" criteria in Augustine and Thomas Aquinas, as well as for the argument for the righteous use of the sword by properly instituted temporal rulers according to Martin Luther's teaching about the two kingdoms.

In contrast, there has always existed in the church a segment that has appealed to the teachings of Jesus, especially in the Sermon on the Mount. "Blessed are the peacemakers" (Matthew 5:9); turn the other cheek. (Matthew 5:39).; and "Love your enemies" (Matthew 5:44). Those who stress this interpretation claim that the true Christian response to violence lays in pacifism and non-violent strategies for resolving conflict.

While it is clear that the majority of Christians after the time of Constantine have adhered to some version of "just war" thinking, there has always coexisted within Christianity the significant presence of principled pacifists. That is still the case in the church today. What is most amazing is how both views—as divergent as can be—preserve a constructive tension that calls the church to responsibility during times of conflict. Somehow we allow for both views to occupy a legitimate place within the spectrum of what it means to be Christian.

Historic Episcopacy?

The recent debate in the ELCA over the full communion proposal with the Episcopal Church, *Called to Common Mission*, is also instructive. [47] This controversy has involved conflicting interpretations, not so much of the Bible as about the correct understanding of the Lutheran confessions. Opponents of the full communion proposal with the Episcopal Church have appealed to Article 7 of the Augsburg Confession: "It is enough (*satis est*) for the true unity of the church to agree concerning the teaching of the gospel and

---

47. *Called to Common Mission: A Lutheran Proposal for a Revision of the Concordat of Agreement,* an agreement of full communion with the Episcopal Church, as amended and adopted by the Churchwide Assembly of the Evangelical Lutheran Church in America on August 19, 1999.

the administration of the sacraments. It is not necessary that human traditions, rites, or ceremonies instituted by human beings be alike everywhere." According to this interpretation, Article 7 precludes the return to historic episcopacy and requiring the sign of apostolic succession through the laying on of hands by bishops at ordinations.

Supporters of *Called to Common Mission* appealed to the Lutheran confessions in a contrasting way, arguing that is was by historical accident that some Lutheran churches fell out of historic episcopacy to begin with, while other Lutheran churches (for example, in Sweden) have preserved this sign. In this view, historic episcopacy appears to be a matter of *adiaphora* that the ELCA is free to choose to recover to the sake of the greater unity of the whole church of Christ.

In this controversy, it is important to note both how the church at assembly opted for the second understanding, yet at the same time introduced a "conscience clause," that in principle allows room for those who adhere to the first interpretation of the confessions. One of the most crucial tests of community is how it deals with those who hold minority opinions.

The ELCA stands before a new dilemma in its deliberation over questions pertaining to the place of homosexuals living in same-gender partnerships. As we have seen, one of the most perplexing features of this controversy is the existence of two mutually contradictory ways of interpreting the key texts that are repeatedly cited in this debate. Is there a way for the church to move beyond a choice of one of these alternatives, beyond excluding one or the other?

How Catholic?

As the Lutheran church, like other Protestant denominations, struggles with deeply divisive and controversial issues, a central question confronts us: "How catholic dare we become?" There are three basic ways that a church may choose to deal with conflicting interpretations of Scripture and tradition: *relativism, exclusivism,* and *catholic.*

Relativism

This is the conviction that truth—at least our human grasp of the truth—is finally relative. Every human person has a certain slice of the truth and no one has the whole truth. This means that it is imperative that we respect each and every opinion equally. There are no meta-narratives that provide a universal explanation of the truth. Tolerance, according to some forms of relativism, is the greatest of virtues. The only limit to tolerance involves the condemnation of all views that are themselves intolerant. There are many Christians today, including many Lutherans, who fear that their church has fallen prey to relativism. This is frequently the charge that is made against mainline churches by the most rapidly growing segment of Christianity in the evangelical and Pentecostal churches.

Exclusivism (or sectarianism)

This is historically the most common Protestant approach to dealing with differences. It is based on the conviction that our community has a privileged access to the truth. Christians have used a number of different standards to measure the truth.

- The literal meaning of Scripture as the Word of God.

- The fundamental tenets of doctrine (such as the virgin birth, miracles, substitutionary atonement, and bodily resurrection).

- The infallibility of the teaching authority of the church's leader (for example, the pope speaking *ex cathedra*).

- Subscription to particular documents of faith that emerged during times of urgent confessing (such as the Lutheran confessions or the Barmen Declaration).

- A particular canon of scriptural truth that norms the entire canon (in other words, a canon within the canon). These canons have varied according to the respective denomination.

Within the last point on page 44, it is fascinating to consider how different denominations appeal to different scriptural warrants.

Roman Catholics appeal to the Petrine principle and teachings about seven sacraments as the basis for ecclesiology.

Lutherans propose the doctrine of justification that we are saved by grace through faith in Christ alone.

The *Reformed* tradition references that God's glory is in God's covenant with humanity in the coming of Christ.

Anglicans affirm that the unity of Christ's church is manifest in its liturgy with a sign of that unity in the practice of the historic episcopacy through the laying on of hands.

Methodists stress the power of the Holy Spirit to work sanctification and holiness in the lives of Christians.

Baptists insist on a believer's baptism as a sign of accepting Jesus Christ.

For *Pentecostals* the Holy Spirit works in the lives of believers through healing, miracles, and speaking in tongues.

Adventists emphasize Christ's second coming and reading the signs of the end times.

For most of Christian history, and especially Protestant history, the exclusivist approach has been lived out by stressing what makes us different from each other, rather than what we hold in common. This has resulted in sharp polemics between those who operate according to different standards of truth. Often within denominations it has led to schism. Wherever disagreements arose about the correct interpretation of the truth, some people would break away to start a new congregation or a new denomination. In the most extreme cases, the exclusivist approach has led to persecutions and violence against those who failed to conform to a particular standard of truth.

Catholic

The catholic approach is based on commitment to certain core essentials of the faith, while allowing a range of views on non-essentials. The key to this approach, of course, is the capacity to reach agreement on what is essential and to let that suffice as the basis of unity, while permitting a range of views on what is deemed non-essential. The Lutheran proposal regarding what is essential to the core of church identity is the doctrine of justification by grace through faith in Christ alone. Over the centuries this proposal has often been applied in an exclusivist way, insisting on agreement about every aspect of doctrine, rather than allowing differences of opinion on adiaphora. In many ways, the controversial issues under debate in the ELCA are a test of our catholicity: Are we clear about what constitutes the center of the Christian faith? How much diversity of opinion is permissible in non-essentials?

The ecumenical movement that gained momentum in the second half of the twentieth century can be viewed as the long overdue attempt on the part of fragmented Protestant traditions to recover their catholicity. It is not accidental that this effort to recover a greater sense of catholic breadth has been occurring exactly at the moment in history when the hegemony of Christendom has been coming to an end. As long as the assumption prevailed that Western society was Christian, the Protestant churches could afford to stress their differences, in competition with one another for members and support. Now that we can no longer assume that society is even faintly based on Christian foundations, it has become urgent for separated churches to demonstrate a greater measure of unity in order that the scandal of division is eliminated and common strategies be devised to serve Christian mission in a post-Christian society.

In the ecumenical process, churches have been challenged to examine ancient causes for division through the development of new hermeneutical methods.[48] The separated churches have been

---

48. *The Condemnations of the Reformation Era: Do They Still Divide?* Ed. Karl Lehmann and Wolfhart Pannenberg, trans. Margaret Kohl (Minneapolis: Fortress, 1990), p. 8.

challenged to ask whether the historic condemnations of the Reformation period still apply to the teachings of the respective other churches as they exist today.[49] In the case of the Reformed churches in their understandings of justification, the sacraments, and the ministry, the ELCA has come to the conclusion that the former condemnations no longer apply. In the case of the Roman Catholic Church, the agreement is even more dramatic. We have even come to the point where together the Roman Catholic Church and worldwide Lutheranism affirm a common understanding of what it means to be justified by grace through faith in Christ.[50] The mutual condemnations at the time of the Reformation about this core Lutheran teaching are no longer valid when applied to the official teachings of our respective churches today. Moreover, "a consensus in basic truths of the doctrine of justification exists between Lutherans and Catholics."[51]

In a new hermeneutical move, we have begun to recognize what were once church-dividing differences as historically conditioned modes of understanding. Whereas once we hurled mutual anathemas at each other, we are beginning to recognize frames of reference that are complementary rather than mutually exclusive.

What do these ecumenical advances in hermeneutical understanding mean for us today, especially in the face of controversial issues? As we seek to negotiate our way through issues that threaten to divide, we are challenged to discover anew our identity as a catholic church. Historically, we Lutherans have tended to define ourselves negatively. We are "Pro-test-ants" after all, defined by what we protest. For example, we are not Catholic, not Reformed, not Anabaptist. This tendency has led to a strong sectarian tendency among Lutherans, whereby we often have been quick to build walls of separation and slow to build bridges of reconciliation. Instead of clearly focusing on our positive and evangelical commitment to

---

49. Ibid., pp. 15-28.

50. *The Lutheran World Federation and The Roman Catholic Church, Joint Declaration on the Doctrine of Justification* (Grand Rapids: Eerdmans, 2000).

51. Ibid., "Official Common Statement," p. 41.

proclaim the saving gospel of Jesus Christ, we have gotten side-tracked into controversy over penultimate issues.

Today when we are faced with the threat of schism due to conflict over deeply controversial issues, we must ask ourselves the question: "How catholic dare we become?" Do we really believe that it is justification by grace through faith in Christ that creates our unity and directs our mission as a church? How broad a range of viewpoints can we allow in penultimate matters?

For example, in the contest between proponents of "just war" theory and proponents of principled pacifism, we have become willing to allow for catholic breadth to encompass these dramatically divergent views. Likewise with reference to the *Called to Common Mission* full communion agreement with the Episcopal Church, we have allowed for a certain range of opinion as befits a catholic church, both the majority position of the ELCA Churchwide Assembly in favor of a process for re-entering the historic episcopacy and a conscience clause for those who hold serious objections.

We now stand before a potentially more divisive issue regarding the church's possible blessing of committed same-gender partnerships and the ordination of persons in such committed same-gender partnerships. Is there an umbrella that can embrace a wide range of views, including what I have called the two irreconcilable hermeneutics? How catholic dare we become?

Questions for Reflection

For personal reflection

1. How do you respond when there is conflict in the church?

2. What does the word *catholic* mean to you when talking about the church? Has your definition changed over the years?

For group discussion

1. What are some of the ways people engage in conflict?

2. What is the difference between the terms *catholic* and *relativism*? Between *catholic* and *exclusivism*?

3. How do we decide whether a particular idea does not belong in the church?

Lord, You Give the Great Commission

With One Voice # 756

Lord, you give the great commission: "Heal the sick and preach the Word."
Lest the Church neglect its mission, and the gospel go unheard,
help us witness to your purpose with renewed integrity.

Refrain
With the Spirit's gifts empow'r us for the work of ministry.

Lord, you call us to your service: "In my name baptize and teach."
That the world may trust your promise, life abundant meant for each,
give us all new fervor, draw us closer in community.

Refrain

Lord, you make the common holy: "This my body, this my blood."
Let us all, for earth's true glory, daily lift life heavenward,
asking that the world around us share your children's liberty.

Refrain

Lord, you show us love's true measure: "Father, what they do, forgive."
Yet we hoard as private treasure all that you so freely give.
May your care and mercy lead us to a just society.

Refrain

Lord, you bless with words assuring: "I am with you to the end."
Faith and hope and love restoring, may we serve as you intend
and, amid the cares that claim us, hold in mind eternity.

Refrain

4

Beyond Polarization to Common Ground

FOSTERING CHARITY

B eing right is not the most important thing in the world. Being charitable is. At least this is the wisdom of the apostle Paul as he wrote to the deeply conflicted congregation at Corinth. In the first letter to the Corinthian church, Paul addressed a series of issues about which he himself held strong opinions. The members of the church were deeply polarized as a complicated set of divisive issues plagued them. These concerns included a case of incest, sexual immorality, the role of marriage, the issue of bringing lawsuits against other members of the church, the practice of eating meat that had been sacrificed to idols, the ordering of spiritual gifts, and the nature of the resurrection. The disorder in the Corinthian church culminated in an irregular celebration of the Lord's Supper, when elite members of the congregation separated themselves from the rest as they shared a meal.

Paul has incisive words to speak regarding each of these problems, conditioned by his commitment to the centrality of the cross and resurrection of Jesus Christ. He charts a course for what he sees as the correct line of action. Paul is never one to mince words. But then he does something extraordinary, out of character, something that undoes even his own sharp rhetoric. He writes a chapter extolling love as the greatest gift.

In other words, the contemporary church is not the first to face intense conflicts. What exacerbates contemporary conflict, however, is a "rhetoric of polarization" that frames our discourse. As humans, we are often both repelled and fascinated by conflict, and the popular media often appeal to this fascination. For example, news programs often place two diametrically opposed views against one another to display the basis of a controversial topic. In order to communicate rapidly and with the greatest emotional appeal, news reports usually do not present a wide range of positions or the nuances of complicated issues. As a result, extreme points of view receive a disproportionate amount of attention. Therefore, I might be tempted to make excessive claims because these will be more likely to draw media attention, without troubling myself about the effect my words will have on those who will hear them. We face today a monumental question: Can we in the church move beyond the "rhetoric of polarization" to abide by a "rhetoric of charity"?

Toward Common Ground

I have argued that the standard approaches to interpreting the disputed biblical texts and the scientific evidence are not likely to move us forward in negotiating questions about homosexuality. Construing the matter as a choice between one of two biblical hermeneutics or between one of two scientific explanations will only lead to further polarization in the church, and eventually to schism in some form. Is there any common ground we can discover under our feet that can serve as the foundation for a more conciliatory outcome? Agreement on the following three points seems to me requisite for establishing such a common ground.

First, all parties need to be clear about the terms of the decision before us. When the church discusses the possibility of blessing committed same-gender relationships and rostering/ordaining otherwise approved persons living in a committed same-gender relationship, many other questions are excluded from consideration. The church has spoken decisively about sexual and emotional behaviors that Christians have deemed sinful, including: adultery; physical, verbal, psychological, or emotional abuse; rape or other non-consensual sexual activity; sexual harassment; promiscuity; prostitution; practices that spread sexually transmitted diseases; pornography; and exploitation of sexuality in the media and advertising.[52] In addition, the church condemns the many forms of commercial sexual exploitation, including viewing pornographic videos, downloading pornography from the Internet, visiting strip clubs, engaging in simulated sex by phone or computer, using escort services, and participating in sex tourism. [53]

All forms of manipulative, exploitative, abusive, and violent sexuality are unacceptable. This includes a severe prohibition against pedophilia and all forms of sexual contact with children. None of these practices is acceptable for Christians, whether homosexual or heterosexual. None of these practices is up for discussion. The question under consideration is actually quite specific. It involves the status of mutually consenting adults of same-gender sexual orientation who desire to live in a committed same-gender relationship. I interpret this to mean a committed lifelong relationship. If we are to discover common ground in the current debate, all parties need to be honest about the specific practice that is being discussed and not confuse the matter with the many other sexual behaviors that are condemned by the church.

Second, we need to center our thinking on the gospel of Jesus Christ. The mission of the gospel, that we are justified by grace through faith for the sake of Jesus Christ, is the ultimate reason for the church's existence. While difficult social issues are important, they remain penultimate concerns. It would be a salutary development if the church were to begin to examine every issue on the table primarily according to the implications for its mission of proclaiming the gospel of Jesus Christ in the world. How might the question of committed same-gender relationships be evaluated according to the criterion of furthering the church's mission of the gospel? I will offer my proposal in this chapter.

Third, even in the face of sharp disagreement over this or other matters, we must relate to one another with deep respect. The

---

52. Cf. "Sexuality: Some Common Convictions," a message adopted by the Church Council of the ELCA on November 9, 1996, pp. 5-7.

53. Cf. "Commercial Sexual Exploitation," a message adopted by the Church Council of the ELCA on November 11, 2001.

decision about the place of committed same-gender relationships is carried out in a church in which each one of us is a baptized child of God. Although viewpoints are diverse and emotions run high, it is imperative for us to acknowledge that those who disagree with us remain Christians. I hope to have made this reality more acute by making the case that the Bible can be interpreted with legitimacy by those who hold diametrically opposing views on homosexuality. There is not one exclusively valid way of interpreting the Scriptures on this matter. The Bible also belongs to those with whom you have strong disagreement. This recognition forces a reconfiguration of the fault lines. There is not just one Christian position. This is a conversation among Christians who hold different views and come to different conclusions even about the scriptural evidence.

A Proposal on Committed Same-Gender Relationships and the Mission of the Church

What might a missionary-centered proposal for negotiating the debate over the blessing of committed same-gender relationships and the rostering/ordaining of approved candidates in such relationships look like? I will outline my thinking on this subject in this chapter. Then I will discuss the importance of pastoral leadership and congregational process in dealing with controversial questions in chapter 5. I offer this proposal not to foreclose on the study currently before the church, but to stimulate the imagination of others about how we together might envision new possibilities beyond either-or decisions. I am very open to critique and hearing other creative proposals for a way beyond the apparent impasse. Martin Marty has quipped that there are billions of possible neural paths within the human brain, meaning that there are also countless new ideas that have yet to have been thought.

My primary theological concern in the debate over any issue is maintaining the centrality of the mission of the gospel. Whenever we devote extraordinary attention to a divisive issue, the danger is that the church's primary mission of proclaiming and witnessing to the gospel of God's grace in Jesus Christ gets sidetracked. This has happened too often in recent years, and there is a strong probability that this will happen again in the present debate over homosexuality. The devil must delight to see the church devouring itself in acrid controversy rather than bearing the gospel to the world.

When we speak of committed same-gender relationships, it is important that we be clear about what we mean. When I employ this term, I take it to mean lifelong committed same-gender relationships.[54] I do not think it wise to use the word *marriage* to describe such relationships. In the Bible and Christian tradition, marriage refers to the commitment of a man and woman for life, out of which relationship biological children might be born. Perhaps the term "committed partnership" should be used instead. The core idea, analogous to marriage, is that the partner provides a stable spiritual, emotional, and sexual companion for the sharing of one's life.

For those who conclude, as do the proponents of the contextual hermeneutic, that the Bible does not condemn homosexuality in a mutually committed relationship between two adults, this still does not mean that the blessing of committed partnerships by the church is morally justified.[55] One would need to make the additional case that enforced celibacy for persons of homosexual orientation is unjust. One would need to allow that a homosexual person has the same right to a partner for life, as do heterosexuals.[56] One would

---

54. For this and the following, cf. Herbert W. Chilstrom and Lowell O. Erdahl, *Sexual Fulfillment—For Single and Married, Straight and Gay, Young and Old* (Minneapolis: Augsburg, 2001), pp. 108-110.

55. See Andrew Sullivan, ed., *Same-Sex Marriage: Pro and Con—A Reader* (New York: Vintage Books, 1997) for a range of arguments about what I am calling "committed same-gender partnerships."

56. Cf. John Witte, *From Sacrament to Law: Marriage, Religion, and Law in the Western Tradition* (Louisville: Westminster John Knox, 1997), pp. 42-73 on Luther's view of marriage as a "social estate."

Cf. M. Mahan Siler Jr., "Same-Gender Covenants," in Walter Wink, ed., *Homosexuality and Christian Faith: Questions of Conscience for the Churches* (Minneapolis: Fortress, 1999), pp. 128-131.

perhaps add the argument that the failure of the church and society to sanction committed partnerships is a key factor in contributing to the instability of relationships in the gay community. Indeed, each of these argument have been made by those who advocate the blessing of committed same-gender partnerships.[57] I would like to underscore my conviction that within such a committed partnership there would need to exist the commitment to lifelong fidelity between partners, including fidelity in sexual intimacy. All forms of promiscuity are precluded within the scope of such a commitment. One of the gifts of a committed partnership would be companionship in facing the vicissitudes of life, loneliness among them.

As a possible outcome to the current study process, I would propose a course of action by which the ELCA would allow individual congregations a measure of autonomy in reading their own context for mission. This is consistent with the conclusion that the biblical witness warrants differences of opinion in interpreting the morality of homosexuality today. With regard to the blessing of committed same-gender partnerships, an individual congregation might be allowed to designate itself as prepared to offer such services of blessing, should it deem this is vital to its missionary outreach. Consistent with the traditional hermeneutic, no congregation would be compelled to adopt such a practice. In many places the issue would not arise as a dimension of congregational mission. In some places the practice of blessing same-gender partnerships may be a key element in congregational mission strategy. Perhaps a three-quarters or larger majority might be required for a congregation to adopt this practice. In effect this proposal would permit individual congregations to self-designate, following guidelines that would be established by the whole church. The practice of offering blessings is already occurring in the ELCA in many places, yet without sanction.

---

57. For a summary of arguments in favor of committed same-gender partnerships, see Patricia Beattie Jung, "Blessing Same-Sex Marriages," *Word and World* 23 (Winter 2003):57-67.

Were the ELCA to permit self-designated congregations to perform blessing services, the church would need to give careful attention to the regulation of standards. Study materials might be made available to congregations desiring to examine the possibility of offering "blessing" services. Guidelines for the preparation of persons for such services of blessing might be developed. Liturgical materials appropriate to such a rite might be prepared. Churchwide materials would need to stress the voluntary nature of this self-designation by congregations. It would become a local option in carrying out congregational mission in a particular context.

This leads to the related consideration of rostering/ordaining otherwise approved candidates who are in committed same-gender partnerships. Again I can imagine a policy whereby the ELCA would allow a measure of congregational autonomy in calling a candidate who is otherwise approved but living in a committed same-gender partnership. In the case of the calling of an ordained person, there may exist a variety of situations where a congregation would declare its openness to or preference for such a pastor. I would hope that serious reflection on the mission of the congregation would be essential in making such a determination. This innovation would entail at least two important procedures.

First, in preparing its paperwork prior to the interviews leading to the call of a new pastor, a congregation would need to indicate its openness to or preference for a pastor living in a committed same-gender partnership.

Second, the ELCA would need to maintain a record of rostered persons who are living in committed same-gender partnerships. In no way would any congregation be forced to accept a candidate living in a committed same-gender partnership against its will. Such a policy would, however, foster honesty in the call process and allow the rostering/ordination of homosexual persons in committed same-gender partnerships for serving certain calls in self-designated congregations.

Additionally, I believe that it is a relative moral good for pastors to offer a blessing to lifelong committed same-gender partnerships rather than requiring that homosexual people either behave as though they are heterosexual or remain celibate. I am fully aware that many objections can be raised to these ideas, yet I believe these conclusions are warranted by the existence of the two irreconcilable hermeneutics for interpreting the contested biblical passages. This proposal attempts to honors both of the contested hermeneutical paradigms.

One danger of this proposal is how it could force individual congregations into divisive controversy, should it be left to the congregation to self-designate in allowing blessing services or calling a person in a committed same-gender partnership. One might contend that this approach abdicates the responsibility of the whole church for making a decision, shifting the burden to the local level. I recognize very acutely the potential for local conflict. I have served as a parish pastor long enough to see this danger clearly. This approach, however, seeks to acknowledge the deep divisions that already exist in the church on this subject, including the two irreconcilable paradigms of interpreting the Bible. It would allow for local assessment of the mission situation. Were a three-quarters or larger majority necessary for a congregation to take these actions, a strong consensus would need to be present on the local level before any action could be taken.

Perhaps the most severe test of this proposal, or any other proposal that allowed for local freedom of debated issues, would be the willingness of congregational members holding the traditional hermeneutic to continue to belong to a church that allowed on any level the blessing of committed same-gender partnerships and the rostering/ordaining of otherwise approved candidates in committed same-gender partnerships for ministry. Much of the outcome would depend on the capacity of our common conviction about justification by grace through faith in Christ alone as sufficing to hold the church together.

Paul reminded the Corinthian congregation in the midst of their multiple controversies that there are many gifts in the church but "the greatest of these is love" (1 Corinthians 13:13). Paul wrote in that same chapter some other lines pertinent to our search for common ground in the matters confounding us today:

. . . as for knowledge, it will come to an end. For we know only in part, and we prophesy only in part; but when the complete comes, the partial will come to an end. When I was a child, I thought like a child, I reasoned like a child; when I became an adult, I put an end to childish ways. For now we see in a mirror, dimly, but then we will see face to face. Now I know only in part; then I will know fully, even as I have been fully known.

— 1 Corinthians 13:8-12,

The New Testament and Psalms: An Inclusive Version

Being right is not the most important thing in the world. All of our knowledge is presently incomplete. The most important thing of all is charity.

Questions for Reflection

For personal reflection

1. On a scale with "being charitable" on one end and "being right" on the other end, where would you place yourself?

2. How could allowing the blessing of committed same-gender partnerships hinder or help the mission of the church?

For group discussion

1. Why is it important that the church be clear that certain sexual practices are sinful and unacceptable?

2. What problems do you see for the proposal about committed same-gender partnerships presented in this chapter? What are the strengths of the proposal?

3. Should a congregation be allowed to offer blessing to committed same-gender partnerships? To call an otherwise qualified pastor who is living in such a partnership?

I, the Lord of Sea and Sky
Here I Am, Lord

With One Voice # 752

I, the Lord of sea and sky, I have heard my people cry.
All who dwell in dark and sin my hand will save.
I, who made the stars of night, I will make their darkness bright.
Who will bear my light to them? Whom shall I send?

Refrain
Here I am, Lord. Is it I, Lord? I have heard you calling in the night.
I will go, Lord, if you lead me. I will hold your people in my heart.

I, the Lord of snow and rain, I have borne my people's pain.
I have wept for love of them. They turn away.
I will break their hearts of stone, give them hearts for love alone.
I will speak my word to them. Whom shall I send?

Refrain

I, the Lord of wind and flame, I will tend the poor and lame.
I will set a feast for them. My hand will save.
Finest bread I will provide till their hearts be satisfied.
I will give my life to them. Whom shall I send?

Refrain

5

Beyond Fear to Mutuality

ATTENDING TO CONGREGATIONAL PROCESS

This chapter offers guidelines for holding conversations about homosexuality in local congregations. Pastoral leadership is instrumental for establishing a climate in which constructive discussion of controversial issues may take place. While the structure of a congregational process may take a variety of forms, it is of utmost importance that the leaders pay attention to process and not just to content. The suggestions that follow are intended to be useful either to an individual congregation ready to enter into an educational forum or to a cluster of congregations desiring to work together in such a process.

The Role of Pastoral Leadership

Pastoral leadership is crucial for the well-being of congregational life. This is all the more true when pastoral leadership involves helping a congregation deal with controversial issues. The office of Word and Sacrament entails great responsibility for the preaching and teaching that takes place in a congregation. Significant influence is exercised over the spiritual lives of the members entrusted to one's care. In the exercise of pastoral leadership, much depends on the creation of a relationship of trust between pastor and people. The mission of a congregation thrives all the more where the members of that congregation know that their pastor loves them.

In dealing with controversial issues, pastoral leadership requires two basic characteristics.[58] First, one must "stay in touch" with the people of the congregation. This means that the pastor must reassure

---

58. These two principles are adapted from family systems theory.

congregation members that disagreement about a particular issue does not undo one's basic attitude of care and concern for them. That we—regardless of our views on a controversial issue—are above all united by God's love for us is the *sine qua non* of entering into honest discussion of divisive issues. If a strong relationship of trust does not exist between pastor and people, this will become all too apparent in the emotional reactions of people to differences of opinion with their pastor. Most people care very much what their pastor thinks. Sometimes the pastor's views can be taken as a sign of God's own position. A pastor needs to be extra sensitive in demonstrating pastoral care and concern for those persons with whom the most serious disagreement exists.

Second, a pastor is wise to make a clear, non-anxious statement of how she or he views a particular issue. In doing so, the use of "I" statements is very important. One can state how "I" come to a certain viewpoint, while making it clear that other people are free to evaluate the evidence for themselves, coming to their own conclusions. This means that a pastor honors the freedom of others to come to a conclusion that is different from the pastor's own view. It also means that in dealing with controversial issues that one avoids defining any one viewpoint as *the* Christian or *the* Lutheran position. By taking a clear, non-reactive position on a given issue, this allows others the freedom to take their own stances. Obviously, this approach is not a formula for controlling the debate and the final outcome. But it is an approach that contributes to healthy community.

This twofold strategy for pastoral leadership in the face of controversial issues avoids two common pitfalls of moral deliberation in the congregation. On the one hand, it puts the well-being of relationships ahead of the need to be right. The reason a particular issue is controversial in the first place is because there is more than one way of looking at it. This approach, following that of Paul in 1 Corinthians, values the health of the community by clearly communicating our care for one another in Christ, regardless of whether we do or do not agree on any given issue. Too often the need to be "right" has destructive consequences for human relationships. On the other hand, this approach also avoids the danger of never being willing to state one's convictions. It is valuable for congregational members to know how their pastor looks at a given subject, as long as they also know that they do not necessarily have to agree with that position.

Perhaps the most destructive form of pastoral leadership in facing controversial issues is one that misrepresents the views of others, allowing no room for differences of opinion in opposition to one's own conclusions. Because pastors are in positions of incredible influence and trust, it is vital that they fairly represent even the positions of those with whom they are in severe disagreement. In cases where the disagreement exists between a pastor and the synod/church body, this means practicing the art of loyal dissent. Where conflict is severe, this could mean choosing to place a higher value on preserving the unity of the church than on insisting upon the rightness of my cause. Choosing the posture of loyal dissent (rather than the posture of schism) is a sign of utmost integrity and love for the church.

Congregational Process

How can a congregation fruitfully conduct moral deliberation of troubling and divisive social issues? As mentioned before, a climate of trust is fundamental for a constructive process. When preparing to discuss a controversial issue in the congregation, it is wise to carefully select a leadership team to work together on the planning. The members of the leadership team should be people who are well respected in the congregation and who have the health of the congregation as their central motive for getting involved. They should be people who represent a range of views on the subject under discussion. They should be good communicators who can give a positive interpretation of the process. They should be ready to commit to several planning meetings in preparation for the congregational sessions.

At every step in the planning process, it is important for members of the leadership team to be prayerful. It is a fearful thing to risk differences of opinion with fellow members of the church and we need to beseech God for guidance and help all along the way. At the beginning of the planning sessions, the leadership team should spend some significant time coming to a consensus about the purpose of the congregational sessions. Is the primary purpose about being a caring community? Is it about the mission of the congregation? Is it about learning to respect those who are different and hold different views? The leadership team in my own congregation settled on two central purposes: 1) To listen to a variety of viewpoints, and 2) to dedicate significant time to small group discussion of predetermined questions (three or four participants assigned to a group randomly). Once the leadership team has devised a statement of purpose, it will be important to return to this expressed purpose repeatedly in the planning to measure whether the team is maintaining focus.

There is an immense amount of material written on the topic of homosexuality and the church. Likewise there are a number of curriculum resources.[59] In our congregation, a reading list was prepared that included titles covering a considerable range of opinion on the subject. Information about various titles was shared mutually among members of the leadership team. The bibliography was then made available to participants in the study series. In designing our curriculum, we decided to pick and choose ideas from several different resources for structuring our sessions. To adequately accomplish the purposes that we set for ourselves within the particular time frame available, our leadership team decided on holding six sessions for congregation members.

---

59. The following resources are available at at www.elca.org/faithfuljourney /resources.html

Journeying Together Faithfully, Part One: ELCA Studies on Sexuality (2002). A four-session study to help congregations and others discuss the ELCA's "Message on Sexuality: Some Common Convictions."

Journeying Together Faithfully, Part Two: The Church and Homosexuality (2003). A six-session study to help congregations and others discuss the church and homosexuality.

Talking Together as Christians about Homosexuality: A Guide for Congregations (Division for Church in Society, 1999). This resource includes a participant's book, leader's guide, and videotape.

Because of the challenging nature of the subject matter, our leadership team agreed to invite a moderator from outside the congregation to facilitate the six sessions. For some congregations, a neighboring pastor might be prepared to serve as a moderator for another congregation. This would free both the church staff (including pastors) and all members of the congregation for participating as inquirers in the study process. One of the key tasks of the moderator is to establish the guidelines for safe learning environment for all participants. In my experience, the moderator was selected as someone who was both knowledgeable on the subject and known for fairness in dealing with others.

At the first session, it is wise to suggest some general rules to follow for how to discuss controversial issues in the church.[60] These include respect for the other, active listening, and using "I" messages. The group might be led to covenant around several basic rules. Because it is likely some new faces will appear at each of the subsequent sessions, it would be useful to reiterate the rules at the start of each gathering.

In speaking with others about a difficult issue like homosexuality, we need to realize how much there is to disagree about.[61] Scripture, tradition, experience, and reason each provide significant areas for serious differences of opinion. It is especially tragic for Christians to denounce those who take an opposing view as being less—or other—than Christians themselves. Each of us holds a partial picture of the full truth and does well to acknowledge the limitations of one's own perspective. When in conversation with someone who takes a contrasting view, it is crucial that we make extra effort to accurately represent the arguments on the other side.

---

60. "Guidelines for Talking about Homosexuality" (reproducible page) in *Talking Together As Christians about Homosexuality*, p. 53. Cf. also "Guidelines and Agreements for Shared Conversation in Community," in the leader packet of *Dialogue and Discernment: A Process for Shared Congregational Conversation around Homosexuality*, modified version by Ecumenical Ministries of Iowa (August 1999), p. 8.

61. For this and the following, cf. Craig L. Nessan, "Can We Talk? Seven Ways to Talk about Hot Topics without Eating Each Other Up," *The Lutheran*, November 1997, pp. 12-13.

Can the other acknowledge your statement of their views as being accurate?

When all is said and done, we may need to agree to disagree. Threatening to leave the congregation or church body is one of the most destructive of all measures. If we find ourselves in the minority position on the issue, it is noble to practice the art of loyal dissent: "A loyal dissenter continues to speak in opposition to the established practice. But this is done in a spirit of integrity that respects the majority's decision while remaining open to all the evidence."[62] Following the tradition of the apostle Paul, I need to learn to speak the truth (as I see it), but always in loving concern for the other and for the well-being of the community (cf. Ephesians 4:15).

Too often the discussion over homosexuality in the church has come to be characterized as a choice between two views. I hope I have not contributed to perpetuating this impression through my sketch of the two irreconcilable hermeneutics. The more I have worked with the literature and engaged in conversation, however, I have realized that there is a whole spectrum of views on this topic.[63] In planning a congregational study of homosexuality and related issues, I encourage leadership teams as much as possible to avoid structuring the sessions as a choice between two alternatives. The more we succeed at presenting a range of opinions, the less polarized the discussion in the congregation will become. Moreover, there are many important insights and nuances of opinion that get lost when I try to reduce others and myself into membership of one of two camps.

One of the most difficult challenges in planning for a congregational study of the issues surrounding homosexuality involves how to include the testimony of gay and lesbian persons themselves and their family members. A thorough study of the issue cannot fail to take seriously the perspectives of those individuals most affected by the congregational discussion. Matters of confidentiality must

---

62. Ibid., p. 13.

63. Cf. the helpful chart showing a range of moral positions on homosexuality in Patricia Beattie Jung and Ralph F. Smith, *Heterosexism: An Ethical Challenge* (Albany: State University of New York Press, 1993), p. 23.

be taken with utmost caution in inviting gay and lesbian persons (or members of their families) to speak, whether they are members of the congregation or not. Presentations by gay and lesbian persons promise to be emotionally evocative for all participants in the study, requiring especially careful planning of how the conversation is to be conducted in response to such presentations.

Perfect Love Casts out Fear

Some days it seems that fear is the emotion that most controls the church. One fearful circumstance follows another—on the international scene, within the church, and within the local congregation. The ministry of pastors is largely occupied with helping others deal with their fears. The human condition itself is such a fearful thing— measuring our success in comparison to others, experiencing losses of many kinds, not knowing what the future holds in store, dealing with finite bodies and minds, and ultimately facing the reality of death. Church members, like all human beings, respond to their fears in some predictable ways. They threaten to leave the church, or flee into inactivity, or withdraw emotionally. They respond to fear by attacking others (including the pastor) with their words and actions, and by placing blame. They become controlling, trying to predetermine how others think and what decisions get made. If you and I are honest, we will need to admit how much our own lives are driven by fear. We too respond to fear through avoidance behaviors, blaming, and trying to manipulate others.

In the face of many experiences of fear, people want their faith to be reliable, even unshakable. Amid the many instabilities of life, most people do not want issues that they thought were settled, like the place of homosexuals in the church, to become another cause for conflict and for fear. They do not want to imagine the possibility of people they know "coming out" as gay or lesbian. They do not want to contemplate the possibility that one of the loved ones in their own family may be struggling with questions of sexual identity. Perhaps on an unconscious level, they may even want to avoid questions that have uncomfortable implications for thinking about their own sexual identity.

I too find the current study process in the ELCA about the blessing of same-gender relationships and the rostering/ordaining of otherwise approved persons in same-gender relationships as reason for fear. As I look back at my ministry over the last 25 years, there have been repeated reasons for fear in dealing with homosexuality. I have had to face my own fear about my relating to gay and lesbian persons. I have had to deal with angry and fearful responses to the publication of the first draft of a possible social statement on human sexuality in 1993. I have been afraid of the fallout when the congregations to which I have belonged have taken up homosexuality as a topic of study. I have had to consider my response as a pastor to vicious speech and hateful actions against homosexuals in the community where I lived. As a seminary administrator, I am afraid of the consequences of the current study process for the institutions of the ELCA. As a seminary professor, I am afraid to go public with my own views on the subject, for fear of how others will react.

In the four Gospels, Jesus frequently addressed the disciples with these incredible words: "Do not be afraid." In facing the fears of my ministry, I take comfort in the promise that Jesus still desires to remove all reasons for fear. It is because of the power of Jesus' forgiveness and grace, given by his dying on the cross and rising from the dead, that we can surrender our fears. In the words of 1 John: "There is no fear in love, but perfect love casts out fear; for fear has to do with punishment, and whoever fears has not reached perfection in love" (4:18, *The New Testament and Psalms: An Inclusive Version*). Could it be that it is because we are not yet perfected in the love of God in Christ that our lives remain so driven by fear?

As he wrote to the conflicted congregation in Corinth, the apostle Paul indicated that it was love, above all else, that was necessary for this troubled church to negotiate its divisions: "Knowledge puffs up, but love builds up. Anyone who claims to know something does not yet have the necessary knowledge; but anyone who loves God is known by him" (1 Corinthians 8:1-3). As we continue to deliberate the issues surrounding homosexuality in the church today, may God so perfect our love that we place the needs of others before our own needs and place the needs of the weak in high regard (cf. 1 Corinthians 8:9-13).

Questions for Reflection

For personal reflection

1. How do you deal with your fears about what could happen to the church in a time of controversy?

2. How can you be involved in the discussion of homosexuality and the church in the most constructive way?

For group discussion

1. What are some of the fears that surround the church's discussion of homosexuality? The fears of pastors? Of congregational leaders? Of the membership? Of gay and lesbian persons and their families?

2. What qualities of leadership are important when a group negotiates controversial issues?

3. What process should your congregation use when it faces a decision about which people sharply disagree? How can you help make your congregation a safe place to hold discussion?

We All Are One in Mission

With One Voice # 755

We all are one in mission;
we all are one in call,
our varied gifts united
by Christ, the Lord of all.
A single great commission
compels us from above
to plan and work together
that all may know Christ's love.

We all are called to service,
to witness in God's name.
Our ministries are diff'rent;
our purpose is the same:
to touch the lives of others
with God's surprising grace,
so ev'ry folk and nation
may feel God's warm embrace.

Now let us be united,
and let our song be heard.
Now let us be a vessel
for God's redeeming Word.
We all are one in mission;
we all are one in call,
our varied gifts united
by Christ, the Lord of all.

6

Exploring the Possibilities

GIVING PLACE TO EACH OTHER

We are a church challenged by many controversial issues that threaten to divide us. Yet God is a God of ever new possibilities! God gives place at the table to persons with whom I fail to see eye to eye on a host of challenging ethical questions: abortion, gun control, war, and genetic engineering, to name but a few. What holds us together in one church is not finally our unanimity about every ethical challenge but *only* our common conviction that Jesus Christ is Lord and Savior.

It is imperative in this time of dramatic polarization in society that we demonstrate a different way of being community with one another in the church. Is it possible for us to practice the art of being church in such a way that together we cling to what binds us together, while living respectfully with one another in matters of critical difference? Can we learn what it means to be a catholic church, even when the issue is as volatile as the questions surrounding homosexuality?

The argument set forth in the previous chapters leaves many unanswered questions concerning the topic of homosexuality as it affects the current debate taking place within the ELCA. This closing chapter addresses 15 of the most pressing questions that may occur in the minds of inquiring readers. The questions posed and the preliminary answers that are offered are to some of the most frequently asked questions I have received from others and that remain in my own mind. May this procedure lead us into deeper understanding that we are a church for whom learning is a continuing lifelong process!

With such a strong focus on the gospel of justification by faith as that which holds us together as a church, what is the place of the law for Christian life?

God's law remains an essential component of the Christian life. According to Lutheran tradition, the law serves two main purposes. First, the law provides a structure for us to conduct our lives in a God-pleasing way by preventing us from harming our neighbor. The Ten Commandments remain an important summary of God's law. It is also important for us to have civil laws and criminal laws that regulate how we should relate to each other. Particularly when your personal interests come into conflict with my personal interests, we may need the law to negotiate our differences. Second, the law teaches us that we can never please God by our own works. Whenever we hold up our lives in the mirror of God's law, we discover that we are failed sinners, desperately in need of God's mercy. This second use of the law forces us to recognize our sinfulness and prepares us to receive the forgiveness and grace that God has showered upon us in the coming of Jesus Christ into the world.

The challenge in every age is to continue to refine the law so that it is as equitable and just as possible. God has not provided a single legal code for all time. God has allowed humans to use their best reasoning in designing laws to counteract the abuses that have come to light and to address new situations as they arise. While laws, like the Ten Commandments, should guide our ethical decisions in every age, the specific interpretation of the Ten Commandments has changed over the course of history.

For example, consider how the Sixth Commandment, "You shall not commit adultery" (Exodus 20:14), has been reinterpreted in recent history with the rapid increase in the divorce rate. Where the church once used the Sixth Commandment to forbid divorce and saw all second marriages as breaking this law, there has been an emerging awareness that in some instances divorce is a tragic necessity due to the irreparable harm to those in the relationship. Mercy for the victims of bad marriages has led to a reinterpretation of the law. We no longer view second marriages as a form of adultery.

(Some people may now reasonably ask whether we have become far too lax in this new interpretation and need to reassert the prohibition of adultery in a stronger form.) So the process of the interpretation of the law remains an unceasing responsibility.

The laws governing the place of homosexuals in the church are, analogously, subject to change. This can be seen in the way that most churches now seek to welcome gay and lesbian persons as members, regardless of how they think about the blessing of same-gender partnerships. There was a day not long ago when the church was completely silent about welcoming homosexuals into membership and this silence meant "Stay away!" Now an increasing number of churches are recognizing that it is baptism that makes one a Christian and that homosexuals are as welcome as any other baptized persons. As Christians we seek to be faithful to the laws God has revealed to us from the past, while at the same time using our best reasoning to interpret the application of the law in our present circumstances.

What makes the question about the place of homosexuals in the life of the church so perplexing is that Christians have major differences in how they think the law should be applied in the case of same-gender partnerships. These differences, however, need not divide the church if we can find a way to honor and respect one another in our varying interpretations of the law for our time. Whereas the church has spoken clearly about those sexual practices that are destructive of human relationships, it remains our present challenge to discern what the law should be regarding the blessing of committed same-gender partnerships and the ordination/rostering of persons living in such partnerships.

How significant is Old Testament law for Christians?

The Old Testament law is very important for Christians. We seek to learn God's will for today by understanding how God's will was once revealed to the people of Israel. A problem begins to arise, however, when we see how Jesus interpreted some Old Testament laws in a new way. For example, Jesus chose to disregard certain cleanliness laws (touching lepers) and Sabbath laws (instructing his disciples to pluck grain on the Sabbath) out of his regard for human health and welfare. "The Sabbath was made for humankind, and not humankind for the Sabbath; so the Son of Man is lord even of the Sabbath" (Mark 2:27-28).

One of the major controversies in the earliest church involved the question of whether the Old Testament laws about circumcision should be enforced for the Gentiles who were joining the Christian church. It was not without strife that the church abandoned the need for male Gentile converts to undergo the rite of circumcision (cf. Acts 15:1-35). Interestingly, the church at that time affirmed that the grace of the Lord Jesus sufficed as the basis for church membership. One of the most significant innovations by Christians in relationship to the Old Testament law was the abandonment of the rituals of sacrifice. Christians affirmed that the death of Jesus on the cross was the final sacrifice for sin, valid for all time (cf. Hebrews 10:1-18). This meant setting aside of many Old Testament laws pertaining to priestly sacrifices.

While we should not prematurely dismiss the Old Testament law today, there is ample precedent for Christians to use careful judgment in applying ancient laws to present circumstances. Those Old Testament laws that are reaffirmed in the New Testament should be of particular interest to Christians. But even here we must be cautious. A number of New Testament prescriptions also have been deemed time-conditioned and no longer applicable to the church today, for example, Paul's instructions about head coverings or women remaining silent in church (1 Corinthians 11:5 and 14:35).

As Christians, we are to respect the Old Testament law and to see it as God's will for the people of God at a particular time in history. At the same time we bear responsibility for interpreting the laws of the entire Bible in a way that provides appropriate structure for living our lives today. The interpretation and application of biblical laws always require our best reasoning about what makes for a just and equitable society today.

More than anything else, Christians look to the Old Testament as a witness to God's faithfulness in keeping promises in every age! We see the Old Testament as testimony to God's gospel that remains true to the end of time. Like the New Testament, the central message of the Old Testament is about God's grace and love and forgiveness—and only secondarily about the law.

Does the civil law allow for a congregation to refuse calling someone who is approved for ordination by the church?

Yes. The First Amendment protection of religious freedom grants churches the right to create the rules that govern the qualifications of its clergy. For example, churches that do not ordain women are free to exercise the religious right to an all-male clergy. Even though there exists civil legislation that provides for equal employment practices for women, this does not apply in the case of church leadership, because of the free exercise of religion provision. In a parallel way, the church is free to enact its own set of rules pertaining to the ordaining of pastors on the basis of sexual orientation. The only limit on such freedom would involve the violation of criminal statutes.

Aren't there moments in history when the church finally has to draw the line and say we can go no further?

Clearly there are such moments in Christian history. There have been numerous times when human authorities have not allowed the church to proclaim the gospel of Jesus Christ in freedom. These have been moments when the church has had to decide whether to defy the state in choosing to preach the gospel under threat of punishment and persecution. The blood of Christian martyrs flowed freely in the early church under the persecution of Rome, as well as more recently in Nazi Germany and the Soviet Union under communism. The clearest moments when the church has had to "draw the line" have been in opposition to dictatorial governments that have forbidden the church to tell the story of salvation in Jesus Christ. These have been occasions for the church to define itself as a "confessing church."

This question also gives occasion to explore whether or not ethical matters ever should become a reason for the church to draw the line. This possibility is relatively rare in Christian history. The Lutheran World Federation's decision to declare ending the apartheid system in South Africa a matter of *status confessionis* provides a recent example of "drawing the line." The church judged a particular ethical issue so urgent that it deserved attention at the same level of urgency as the proclamation of the gospel itself. Opposing apartheid was deemed of such importance that it was made into a defining characteristic of Christian faithfulness. Recently, I proposed that ending world hunger be elevated by the churches to become a matter of *status confessionis.*[64] Based on the biblical witness and the intolerable disparity between rich and poor in our contemporary world, I have argued that ending hunger needs to become a core commitment of the Christian church in our time, a matter of "confessing church."

For the church to declare itself in a "state of confessing" with regard to a particular ethical issue requires profound clarity about

---

64. Craig L. Nessan. *Give Us This Day: A Lutheran Proposal for Ending World Hunger* (Minneapolis, Augsburg Fortress, 2003).

the scriptural witness and its meaning for the present. While some make the case that refusing to bless same-gender partnerships should become for the church of the present a matter of *status confessionis*, I would counter that the scriptural witness is far more ambiguous with regard to homosexuality than it is, for example, about racism or hunger. For this reason, I would implore all parties—those who advocate a change in present ELCA policy as well as those who argue for its continuation—to refrain from making this issue a matter for "confessing church." Instead of taking stands that will inevitably lead to schism, I encourage the ELCA to implement a process that allows for studied differences of opinion to coexist. While there may indeed be moments when the church has to "draw a line," I hope and pray that all those who have strong opinions with regard to homosexuality will choose not to do so.

What would need to change officially if the ELCA revised its current policy on blessing same-gender partnerships and ordaining/rostering otherwise qualified persons who are living in such partnerships?

To the best of my knowledge and research, there would need to be no change in the Constitution of the Evangelical Lutheran Church in America. The primary change would need to be made in the policy document, *Vision and Expectations*, in particular the paragraph on sexual conduct. This statement was adopted by the Church Council of the ELCA in October 1990. It is, of course, imperative that any proposed change be deliberated carefully through an intentional study process such as the church is undertaking, under the direction of the Task Force for the ELCA Studies on Sexuality. Because it was a Churchwide Assembly that authorized the work of the task force, it will also be a Churchwide Assembly that receives the report and recommendation of the task force. It is therefore very important that congregations participate now in their own study processes, in order that the members of congregations are prepared to offer their best thoughts to the task force.

If we change the ELCA's policy about blessing same-gender partnerships, are we caving in to the low-ethical standards of our culture?

At first it may appear so. We need to reiterate, however, that the church clearly condemns adultery; physical, verbal, psychological, or emotional abuse; rape or other non-consensual sexual activity; sexual harassment; promiscuity; prostitution; practices that spread sexually transmitted diseases; pornography; and exploitation of sexuality in the entertainment media and advertising.[65] In addition, the church condemns the many forms of commercial sexual exploitation: viewing pornographic videos, downloading pornography from the Internet, visiting strip clubs, engaging in simulated sex by phone or computer, using escort services, and participating in sex tourism.[66] These strong prohibitions establish the basis for very clear Christian standards for sexual ethics.

When we as a church consider the blessing of committed same-gender partnerships, we are deliberating a very particular kind of homosexual relationship. We are not talking about blessing abusive or promiscuous activity, whether heterosexual or homosexual. We are not talking about blessing exaggerated sexual stereotypes some-times associated with gay people. We are talking specifically about the blessing of a lifelong commitment of two mutually consenting adults of homosexual orientation. In some ways, for the church to affirm the blessing of same-gender committed partnerships would be very *counter* cultural! It would ask of gay men and lesbians the same kind of sexual fidelity that it expects of heterosexuals. The church would be setting a clear standard for the type of committed relationships expected of gay men and lesbians, parallel to the expectations for heterosexuals in the church.

---

65. Cf. "Sexuality: Some Common Convictions," a message adopted by the Church Council of the ELCA on November 9, 1996, pp. 5-7.
66. Cf. "Commercial Sexual Exploitation," a message adopted by the Church Council of the ELCA on November 11, 2001.

How can two irreconcilable viewpoints both be accepted by the church?

This is a challenging question. It is helpful to keep in mind that there are already many issues in the church where members hold irreconcilable views. For example, Lutherans have sharp differences of opinion on the topic of abortion. Some hold to an anti-abortion stance while others defend the "pro-choice" position. Similarly, some members of our church are deeply convinced that there are circumstances that necessitate the waging of a "just war," while others argue that the Christian faith necessitates pacifism.

In these and other instances, Christians of deep conviction reason differently about the substance of the faith and come to diametrically opposed conclusions. I have suggested that it is a healthy sign of the catholicity of the church to expect agreement about those matters that are core to the Christian faith (the doctrine that we are justified by grace through faith in Jesus Christ alone), while allowing a range of viewpoints on non-essential matters. Much depends on the ability of the parties that are at odds with each other to acknowledge that the position they hold does indeed involve a matter that is "non-essential." We are sorely tempted to argue that those issues, about which we have the most passion, deserve "core" status, thus elevating them into matters for "confessing church" (*status confessionis*).

An extremely critical question stands before us: Will individuals with deep convictions about what the Bible says about homosexuality be able to acknowledge that those with opposite views do so out of a genuine Christian conviction and therefore deserve our utmost respect? It is my prayer that it will be possible for those with widely varying views on the questions of blessing committed same-gender partnerships and allowing ordained/rostered service for those otherwise qualified candidates living in such relationships to find a way of staying together in the same church. I have been in conversation with many faithful people in different synods of the ELCA, and I believe it will be possible. Not easy, but possible.

What do you mean when you suggest that there are not just two, but rather a spectrum of views on how people look at homosexuality?

The issue of homosexuality has become so polarized that it is easy to think there are only two ways of looking at it; you are either for it or against it. This approach mimics the handling of controversial issues in the media. We hear only about the two extremes in every conflict. While this may make for an interesting 30-second television report, it reduces the complexity of issues and distorts them immensely.

First of all, with regards to homosexuality, there are many ways to view the subject. For those mainly interested in what the Bible says, there are not only the seven texts that make some explicit reference to homosexual relations but also many other texts that could add insight to the current discussion (the decision to include Gentiles in the Christian church without circumcision in Acts 15; Jesus' response to the woman caught in adultery in John 8; Jesus' discussion on divorce in Matthew 19; or Jesus' command to love one's enemies in Matthew 5.)

Depending on which texts you cite, your viewpoint will be different from those who primarily make reference to other Bible passages. Similarly, there are different scientific studies on the causes of homosexual orientation. Depending on which of these studies you hold to be reliable, your own understanding will be shaped differently from someone who reads the evidence from another angle. When we listen carefully to each other, we learn there are not just two ways of reading the Bible or two ways to interpret science but rather many varying ways.

Some views on homosexuality are decisively influenced by what the law says. Depending on how you weigh the significance of the decisions by legislatures and courts, your view of homosexuality is changed. Many pastors and lay people have primary concern for how to offer pastoral care to gay and lesbian persons and their families. They are less concerned about making value judgments and more concerned about how to show God's love to those who are feeling marginalized by the church. Depending on how one approaches pastoral care, one's view of homosexuality becomes nuanced differently. One of the strongest influences on how someone looks at homosexuality is their personal experience with gay and lesbian persons. For those who have a friend or family member who is homosexual, their viewpoint on the general subject of homosexuality cannot help but be influenced by these personal relationships. These examples demonstrate how what you hold to be authoritative shapes your opinion about what stance the church should be taking on homosexuality.

One helpful tool for visualizing the spectrum of conclusions that different people take has been formulated by Patricia Beattie Jung and Ralph F. Smith. They outline not two but five moral positions that are often taken with regard to homosexuality.[67]

Immorality:	Homosexuality is evil.
Alcoholism:	Homosexuality is a disease.
Blindness:	Homosexuality is a defect.
Color blindness:	Homosexuality is an imperfection.
Left-handedness:	Homosexuality is a variation.

This helps us recognize there is a wide range of views about homosexuality and not just two polarized positions. It should assist us in carefully listening to one another as we talk together about homosexuality and avoid prematurely labeling each other according to the prevailing stereotypes.

---

67. For detailed information, see the complete chart in Jung and Smith, *Heterosexism*, p. 23.

How do we take into consideration the views of young people on this subject?

I hope we are listening to people of all ages as we study and come to some proposals about how the church should think about homosexuality. The best way we can engage the views of young people is by taking the time to talk with them and listen to them, taking their perspectives seriously. My own impression is that while some young people have very strong views about the immorality of homosexuality, most young people are growing up in a society where tolerance of more and more differences, including differences about sexual orientation, is simply expected. This has become a very strong value among young people in the United States for the last two generations. Some argue that such tolerance reflects the failure of the church to instill strong Christian values in the young generation.

Another way of interpreting this is to say that young people are grounding their acceptance of different groups of people (including gay and lesbian people) in their understanding of the Christian gospel, that God's love and grace knows no boundaries. Young people who have attended recent synod and churchwide events have been quite articulate and outspoken about the ELCA becoming more accepting of gay and lesbian persons.[68] These youth do not understand why the homosexuality debate is so controversial for many adults. If this is an accurate snapshot of where the church is heading in the next generations, it means that there will be continuing pressure for the church to reexamine its views in the coming years.

---

68. See the resolutions of the 2003 Lutheran Youth Organization convention at www.elca.org/dcm/youth/lyo/convention_highlights.html.

What do you mean by catholic?

I am using the term *catholic* in the same way that we now confess the Nicene Creed: "We believe in one holy catholic and apostolic Church." The term *catholic* is the original word used to describe that the church is universal; that there is one church that exists throughout space and time. While there is much that is culturally different among all the Christians living in the world today, we affirm that we are all part of the one catholic church. Likewise, there is much that is historically different among the Christians who have lived at different times in the past; we affirm that we are united with them in the one catholic church. We make this affirmation not because we have the same worldviews and are in agreement about every ethical issue but because we share the catholic faith in the centrality of Jesus Christ and the salvation that comes through his life, death, and resurrection.

The term *catholic* allows for a spectrum of views on non-essential matters, even while we are held together by the faith which is essential for all—that we are saved by the power of Jesus Christ and by Jesus Christ alone. It is my contention that the ELCA now stands at a crossroads in its history. The time has come for us to decide to be a catholic church. In the past, Lutheran churches often chose to settle differences of opinion by separating into smaller churches where everyone was of the like mind. I call this the "sectarian" approach. It is a strong tendency for Lutherans, often justified with reference to Martin Luther's own cry, "Here I stand, I can do no other." We have been haggling out differences over the last decade, always under the threat of schism. It is my prayer that we can arrive at a new appreciation for the catholic nature of the church, allow the gospel to suffice as the basis for our unity, and live together in the same church with an appreciation for legitimate diversity.

What are the major teachings of the Lutheran church on the subject of homosexuality?

I think it is fair to say that there are no major teachings of the Lutheran church on homosexuality. As explained in the first chapter of this book, the central Lutheran teaching is about justification by grace through faith in Jesus Christ alone. It is somewhat alarming that the centrality of this teaching is not better recognized in the life of the Lutheran church today.

Lutherans also have a major teaching about the authority of the Bible. This does not mean, however, a biblical literalism that reads every verse of the Bible as having equal importance. Lutherans understand that those sections of the Bible that point to the grace, love, and forgiveness of God in Jesus Christ have more significance than any other part. In fact, Lutherans teach that all the rest of the Bible needs to be interpreted on the basis of this gospel message about Jesus Christ.

While Lutherans take very seriously all the verses of the Bible, including those that make explicit reference to homosexual relations, we give first importance to those verses that proclaim what God has done for our salvation by sending Jesus Christ. This means that we properly distinguish between that which points to the gospel of Jesus Christ in the Scriptures and those matters that have to do with the law. While we have freedom to reason about the interpretation of the law, we can only receive as a gift what God has chosen to do for us in the gospel of Jesus Christ.

Predecessor Lutheran church bodies, such as the Lutheran Church in America and the American Lutheran Church, issued statements about human sexuality that prohibited same-gender sexual relationships and affirmed sexual intercourse only within the marriage between a man and woman.[69] This is the antecedent for

---

69. Cf. "Human Sexuality and Sexual Behavior, A Social Statement of The American Lutheran Church," a predecessor church body of the ELCA (1980) and "Sex, Marriage, and Family, A Social Statement of the Lutheran Church in America," a predecessor church body of the ELCA (1970).

the current policy that was adopted by the Evangelical Lutheran Church in America and is set forth in the document *Visions and Expectations: Ordained Ministers in the Evangelical Lutheran Church in America*, adopted by the Church Council in October 1990. This document states:

> Single ordained ministers are expected to live a chaste life. Married ordained ministers are expected to live in fidelity to their spouses, giving expression to sexual intimacy within a marriage relationship that is mutual, chaste, and faithful. Ordained ministers who are homosexual in their self-understanding are expected to abstain from homosexual sexual relationships.[70]

This statement upholds the traditional teaching of the church about homosexuality. While there is no specific Lutheran teaching about homosexuality, the Lutheran church has upheld the traditional teaching as reflected in its current policy. The current conversation in the church centers on the question of whether this policy should be changed, in light of other ways of interpreting Scripture and the present context.

---

70. *Vision and Expectations: Ordained Ministers in the Evangelical Lutheran Church in America* (Chicago: ELCA, 1990), p. 13.

What do you think of Christian ministries that try to change homosexuals into heterosexuals?

First of all, I think that sexual orientation is one of life's mysteries, and we need to be very humble when we speak about it. Many studies suggest that multiple factors contribute to the formation of sexual orientation—genes, hormones, the environment—and each of the factors may contribute to different degrees in the case of a particular individual.

To the degree that one determines that sexual orientation is a result of genetic or prenatal hormonal influences, it seems to me that attempts to "change homosexuals into heterosexuals" are not only futile but morally wrong. Here is where the argument for celibacy is preferable to strategies that would attempt to change what is profoundly embedded in the identity of a person. Here too is where the argument for allowing committed same-gender relationships gains credibility—that it is unjust to deny the possibility of a sexual partner for life to someone who is of homosexual orientation due to "uncontrollable" factors.

On the other hand, to the degree that sexual orientation is a result of environmental or psychological influences, it seems to me that change through counseling might be possible in some cases. The scientific literature about the possibility and success rate of changing sexual orientation is highly contested. Yet because of what I take to be the complexity of factors that influence sexual orientation, I can entertain the possibility that, for select individuals, the Christian ministries described in this question can offer support for those who seek it.

Even as the ministries that encourage changing sexual orientation may be useful for a select number of individuals, they may be harmful for others, increasing guilt and leading to deeper self-negation. Depression and suicide rates are particularly high among adolescents who are struggling with sexual identity, and we need to be sensitive to their mental and spiritual well-being.

As we in the church give guidance to those who are questioning their sexual orientation, especially young people, it is imperative that we treat each individual with respect and listen carefully to each person's story, praying that God will guide us in lending appropriate pastoral counsel.[71] If sexual abuse is part of the story, we need to make referrals to those with particular expertise in helping the victims. Synods can provide the names of counselors in whom the church has confidence in dealing with sexual abuse. We need to pray for the Spirit's guidance as we minister to persons dealing with the complexity of discerning sexual orientation, seeking consultation where we lack expertise for the task, yet preserving the bond of confidentiality.

---

71. Cf. the useful guidance of David K. Switzer, *Pastoral Care of Gay Men, Lesbians, and Their Families* (Minneapolis: Fortress, 1999), pp. 80-100.

Why do people react so strongly to the topic of homosexuality?

Usually the reason people react strongly on any given subject is because of their fear. When we are afraid, we are prone to act in such a way as to protect ourselves from that which is causing the threat. Fear leads to our acting in self-defense and lashing out in anger. In the case of homosexuality, there are fears on every side. Gay and lesbian people are afraid of rejection by their families and by the members of the church. Stories of rejection are many and this fear is based on real and hurtful experience. Those who advocate for gay and lesbian persons are angry about the way the church has dealt with homosexual persons in the past and want to see changes in the church's policy to guarantee full participation and acceptance. They are afraid that the church will lose these gifted people, if they fail to receive a welcome.

Those who oppose changing the church's policy on the blessing of same-gender relationships and the ordination of those in such relationships also have many fears. They fear that this is another instance where the values of unchristian society are taking over the church. They fear the loss of their Christian faith as a foundation they can depend on. They fear we are not being faithful to Scripture.

Much of the fear about homosexuality, I believe, stems from fear for our children. Many are afraid that children will be influenced to become homosexual, if the church were to allow the blessing of same-gender partnerships and the ordination of otherwise qualified persons who are living in such a blessed partnership. There is fear that this development would lead to an increase in the number of young people who are swayed into identifying as gay or lesbian. A prevalent fear of many parents is that one of their own children might have to struggle with questions of sexual orientation, so they want to prevent any external influences from contributing to this possibility.

I also wonder sometimes if some of the strong reactions to the homosexuality debate stem from our own experience of sexual identity. To whatever degree that sexual orientation is deeply engrained in one's own biological makeup, it seems to me natural that heterosexuals would have a strong aversion to the idea of homosexuality. This would be a response hard-wired into heterosexual persons as a provision for the propagation of the human species. By offering this suggestion, I intend no moral judgment. Such an explanation does not mean heterosexuals should feel guilty about their reaction. It should, however, help heterosexuals understand why it might be natural for them to have a hard time understanding homosexual attraction. It runs counter to their own natural sexual attraction. What is more, part of being heterosexual would entail experiencing an aversion to the very notion of homosexual relations.

As with any fear in life that causes deep emotions, we need to examine our fear to see what is based on a reasonable threat and what about our fear needs to be revised, based on closer examination of what can be known about the reason for fear. One potential value of a congregational study process on this topic is that it can allow the opportunity to state openly our fears and get more information for testing whether our fears are truly valid.

How would your proposal change life in my congregation?

It is my prayer that every congregation would be honored by the proposal that congregations have the right to their own decision about performing services of blessing for committed same-gender partnerships and about calling an otherwise qualified pastor who is living in such a committed same-gender partnership. For congregations where a strong consensus exists that the performance of such blessings or the calling of such a pastor fosters their mission, this proposal would allow for these practices to be sanctioned according to the policy established by the church to govern them. Insofar as there already are congregations performing services of blessing and being served by pastors living in committed same-gender relationships (however irregular), this change would provide for a more honest and orderly practice.

In congregations where there is no interest or consensus about introducing these practices, there would be no internal change in the congregation's life together. I want to reiterate that no congregation would be forced into adopting services of blessing or receiving a pastor living in a committed same-gender relationship according to my proposal. In fact, I contend that there should be virtual unanimity in a congregation before any change be introduced. The only change that would affect those congregations maintaining traditional practices is an external one: they would now be in fellowship with congregations that followed a practice different from their own. While this would test the church's unity, it is de facto not so new a situation. Already we coexist in one church where some congregations are in fact performing blessings of committed same-gender relationships and already we coexist with congregations that have dramatically different practices on the ordination question. The allowance for congregational decision would be a form of recognition that we are deeply divided on these questions and respect the diversity that already exists.

Why do you emphasize fear as such an important issue?

The fact that emotions run so very high whenever we begin to discuss the questions surrounding homosexuality leads me to the conclusion that something more than reason is at work in this discussion. This is not to dismiss the fact that there are very different ways of interpreting Scripture and very different forms of reasoning among the various parties in the homosexuality debate. But the volatility of the discussion is an indicator that we are caught up in something that transcends our best critical analysis and reason. Were we as a church to be able to name our fears—accurately and honestly—I cannot help but believe we could come to an agreeable resolution of even this divisive issue. This entire book has been written as a contribution toward this very outcome: the preservation of the unity and the mission of Christ's church.

I close with an admonition from the Letter to the Ephesians:

> But speaking the truth in love, we must grow up in every way into him who is the head, into Christ, from whom the whole body, joined and knit together by every ligament with which it is equipped, as each part is working properly, promotes the body's growth in building itself up in love.
>
> ⸻ Ephesians: 4:15-16, NRSV

May we be such a church—many members, yet one body!

Questions for Reflection

For personal reflection

1. How has your mind changed by reading this book? How has it stayed the same?

2. What do you want to do to learn more about the subject of this book?

For group discussion

1. In what ways do you agree or disagree with the answers given to the questions in this chapter? How would you answer them differently?

2. What further questions do you have that you would like to ask the author?

3. How have you practiced the art of "speaking the truth in love"?

Glossary

Adiaphora: A Latin term for an issue about which church members are free to hold different opinions. A matter that is important but not core to Christian identity.

Barmen Declaration: A statement issued by pastors and lay people at a church gathering held at Barmen, Germany, in May 1934 that sets forth the theological arguments for opposing Hitler's takeover of the Protestant Church.

Contextual hermeneutic: An approach to the interpretation of the Bible that pays decisive attention to the original context when a passage was written and argues that we must seriously consider the differences between the original context and the present context.

Ecclesiology: Literally, "the study of the church." A term that describes a theological understanding of what it means to be the Church.

Eschatology: Literally, "the study of the last things." A term that describes a theological understanding of what will happen at the end of history.

Hermeneutics: A formal approach to interpreting the Bible that bridges its meaning in the ancient world and its meaning for today.

Holiness Code: A major section of the Old Testament, found in Leviticus 17-26, that focuses on what it means for the people of Israel to remain holy before God.

Justification: The central teaching of the Lutheran Church that we receive salvation by grace alone through faith in Jesus Christ, not by our own works.

Lutheran Confessions: A collection of documents from the time of the Reformation that are authoritative for the teachings of the Lutheran Church. Chief among these documents are the Augsburg Confession and Luther's Small Catechism.

anxious presence: A term from family systems theory that describes the most effective way to live in relationship to others. The opposite of reacting anxiously to others.

Pederasty: In the ancient Greek world, a mentoring relationship between an older man and an adolescent male that often included homosexual relations.

Penultimate: If the ultimate refers to that which is the most important of all, the penultimate refers to something very important but not ultimate.

Self-differentiation: A term from family systems theory that describes how one should remain deeply concerned about other people without becoming overly dependent on them. Someone who is self-differentiated both cares about others and at the same time maintains the freedom to hold views that may be different from them.

Status confessionis: A Latin term that describes an urgent situation when something that had been adiaphora now becomes a matter that is considered core to Christian identity.

Traditional hermeneutic: An approach to biblical interpretation that, while considering the original context in which the Bible was written, favors a long-established understanding of Scripture that has developed over the centuries.

Ultimate: That which is the most important of all. Theologically, that which belongs to the very essence of God.

Bibliography

Balch, David L., editor. *Homosexuality, Science, and the "Plain Sense" of Scripture.* Grand Rapids: Eerdmans, 2000.

Brawley, Robert L., editor. *Biblical Ethics and Homosexuality: Listening to Scripture.* Louisville: Westminster John Knox, 1996.

Brooten, Bernadette J. *Love Between Women: Early Christian Responses to Female Homoeroticism.* Chicago: University of Chicago Press, 1996.

Childs, James M., Jr., editor. *Faithful Conversation: Christian Perspectives on Homosexuality.* Minneapolis: Fortress, 2003.

Chilstrom, Herbert W., and Lowell O. Erdahl, *Sexual Fulfillment—For Single and Married, Straight and Gay, Young and Old.* Minneapolis: Augsburg, 2001.

Gagnon, Robert A. J. *The Bible and Homosexual Practice: Texts and Hermeneutics.* Nashville: Abingdon, 2001.

Geis, Sally B., and Donald E. Messer, editors. *Caught in the Crossfire: Helping Christians Debate Homosexuality.* Nashville: Abingdon, 1994.

Grenz, Stanley J. *Welcoming but Not Affirming: An Evangelical Response to Homosexuality.* Louisville: Westminster John Knox, 1998.

Hays, Richard B. *The Moral Vision of the New Testament: Community, Cross, New Creation: A Contemporary Introduction to New Testament Ethics.* San Francisco: HarperCollins, 1996.

Jung, Patricia Beattie, and Ralph F. Smith. *Heterosexism: An Ethical Challenge.* Albany: State of New York Press, 1993.

Nissinen, Martti. *Homoeroticism in the Biblical World: A Historical Perspective.* Minneapolis: Fortress, 1998.

Rudy, Kathy. *Sex and the Church: Gender, Homosexuality, and the Transformation of Christian Ethics.* Boston: Beacon Press, 1997.

Scroggs, Robin. *The New Testament and Homosexuality.* Philadelphia: Fortress, 1983.

Seow, Choon-Leong, editor. *Homosexuality and Christian Community.* Louisville: Westminster John Knox, 1996.

.er, Jeffrey S., editor. *Homosexuality in the Church: Both Sides of the Debate.* Louisville: Westminster John Knox, 1994.

Soards, Marion L., editor. *Scripture and Homosexuality: Biblical Authority and the Church Today.* Louisville: Westminster John Knox, 1995.

Swartley, Willard M. *Homosexuality: Biblical Interpretation and Moral Discernment.* Scottsdale: Herald Press, 2003.

Sullivan, Andrew, editor. *Same-Sex Marriage: Pro and Con. A Reader.* New York: Vintage, 1997.

Swidler, Arlene, editor. *Homosexuality and World Religions.* Valley Forge: Trinity Press International, 1993.

Switzer, David K. *Pastoral Care of Gay Men, Lesbians, and Their Families.* Minneapolis: Fortress, 1999.

Wink, Walter, editor. *Homosexuality and Christian Faith: Questions of Conscience for the Churches.* Minneapolis: Fortress, 1999.

Witte, John. *From Sacrament to Law: Marriage, Religion, and Law in the Western Tradition.* Louisville: Westminster John Knox, 1997.

The following ELCA publications are available on-line at www.elca.org/faithfuljourney/resources.html

Journeying Together Faithfully, Part One: ELCA Studies on Sexuality. Chicago: ELCA Division for Church in Society, 2002.

Journeying Together Faithfully, Part Two: The Church and Homosexuality. Chicago: ELCA Division for Church in Society, 2003.

Talking Together as Christians about Homosexuality. A Guide for Congregations. Chicago: ELCA Division for Church in Society, 1999.